P9-DFX-557

GREAT RAILWAY JOURNEYS ~OF THE~ EAST

GREAT RAILWAY JOURNEYS ~OF THE~ EAST

Evocative accounts of legendary train routes

Max Wade-Matthews

southwater

This edition is published by Southwater

Southwater is an imprint of
Anness Publishing Limited
Hermes House
88-89 Blackfriars Road
London
SE1 8HA
tel. 020 7401 2077
fax 020 7633 9499

Distributed in the UK by
The Manning Partnership
251-253 London Road East
Batheaston
Bath
BA1 7RL
tel. 01225 852 727
fax 01225 852 852

Distributed in the USA by
Anness Publishing Inc.
27 West 20th Street
Suite 504
New York
NY 10011
tel. 1 212 807 6739
fax 1 212 807 6813

Distributed in Australia by
Sandstone Publishing
Unit 1, 360 Norton Street
Leichhardt
New South Wales 2040
Australia
tel. 2 9560 7888
fax 2 9560 7488

All rights reserved. No part of this publication may be reproduced, stored in a retrieval system, or transmitted in any way or by any means, electronic, mechanical, photocopying, recording or otherwise, without the prior written permission of the copyright holder.

© 2000 Anness Publishing Limited

1 3 5 7 9 10 8 6 4 2

Publisher Joanna Lorenz
Project Editor Joanne Rippin
Editor Emma Gray
Designer Michael Morey

Contributors George Behrand, Gary Buchanan, Tom Ferris, Colin Garratt, Alex Grunbach, Frank Hornby, Alan Pike, Graham Pike, Christopher Portway, Brian Solomon, Kenneth Westcott-Jones, Neil Wheelwright

Previously published as part of a larger compendium, *Great Railway Journeys of the World*

Picture Acknowledgements

The majority of the pictures in this book were provided by Milepost 92 1/2. The Publishers would also like to thank the following people and organizations for additional pictures:
Adrian Baker/Photobank: pp105M, 105B, 108B, 108T. Jeanetta Baker/Photobank: pp62T, 63T, 63BR, 65TL, 87T, 89B, 91T, 110T, 111B. Peter Baker/Photobank: pp10T, 10B, 11B, 64T, 65BL, 86B, 88T, 89TL, 90B, 110B. Paul Barney/Travel Ink: p101B. Nick Battersby/Travel Ink: pp24T, 25B. George Behrand: pp25M, 25TL, 26B, 27T, 28T, 30T, 31BL, 32T. Beyer Peacock & Co. Ltd: p18T. Gary Buchanan: pp14BL, 14M, 14BR, 15, 16T, 17T, 19B. Trevor Creighton/Travel Ink: pp98B, 99T, 99BL. A E Durrant: pp16T, 19T. The Eastern and Oriental Express Press Office: pp6, 84T, 85TR, 85B. Abbie Enock/Travel Ink: pp26T, 26M, 27B, 28BL, 29B, 47. Alex Grunbach: pp 96M, 98T, 99BR, 100, 101T, 102TR, 102L, 103T, 104, 105T, 106–7, 108T, 109B, 111T, 112–17. Allan Hartley/Travel Ink: pp44T, 45. G Holland: pp102L, 103B. Brian Lovell: pp82B. Office National des Chemins de Fer, Rabat: pp8–9. Gavin Morrison: pp17TR, 17B, 18B, 34–5. Jeremy Phillips: p101M. Alan Pike: pp86T, 86M, 87M, 87B, 88B, 89TR, 90T, 91B. Graham Pike: pp70–1, 118, 120M, 120B, 121B, 122–7. Christopher Portway: pp37B, 39M, 40T, 42, 43B, 50–5, 66B, 67T. Gordon Smith/Photobank: p110B. Brian Solomon: pp72–5, 82T, 82M, 83. David Toase/Travel Ink: pp36B, 37TR, 38T, 39T, 39B. Max Wade-Matthews: pp10M, 41T. Kenneth Westcott-Jones: pp12–13, 36T, 37M, 38B. Neil Wheelwright: pp20–3, 75–81, 119, 120T, 121T.
Jacket photography provided by Milepost 92 1/2 (front image and back (top right)) and Corbis back (top left)

Contents

● ABOVE

The East African Railways "Mount Blackett" climbs a steep coastal escarpment.

EASTERN & ORIENTAL EXPRESS

Introduction

This book takes the reader on some of the most exciting rail journeys in the world, from the romance of the Trans-Siberian Express to the fabulous luxury of the South African Blue Train. The reader will experience the scorching deserts of Iran and the verdant lands of West Africa. This book also brings to life historical figures such as Lawrence of Arabia whose destruction of the railways in Saudi Arabia still has not been repaired, and we go to China, one of the last bastions of the steam locomotive.

India is not forgotten as we travel the length and breadth of the sub-continent, riding on trains ranging from the luxurious Palace on Wheels to the "toy train" that takes us up the foothills of the Himalayas to the town of Darjeeling. We visit Australia where we remember the pioneers of the 19th century through whose efforts the railways of that vast continent were laid, and lastly New Zealand for, among others, its spectacular Transalpine journey.

● **OPPOSITE**
The Eastern and Oriental Express near Kanchanaburi, Thailand.

● **ABOVE**
The afternoon train leaves Pachegaon station, in India, which amounts to little more than a sign board set amid the scrub.

CASABLANCA TO GABES

● ABOVE
Ouja railway station on the border between Algeria and Morocco.

The trains on this line will take the rail traveller all along the Mediterranean coast of North Africa from Morocco's Casablanca, via Tangier, to Gabes in south-eastern Tunisia, some 1,778 km (1,105 miles) in all. French from 1840 to 1960, Algeria was treated as a *département* of France, and its railway – the Société Nationale des Transports Ferroviaires (SNTF) – was constructed and run accordingly. Built to standard gauge, the trains ran with a pre-war speed and efficiency admired by many countries. The system is basically coastal, to provide a link between Casablanca in Morocco and Tunis, at one time all French.

Neither Moroccan nor Algerian Railways are the slightest mite house-proud. Some of the trains are a disgrace. From Fez to the Algerian border, compartments are a mass of sprawling bodies trying to get some sleep on wooden seats.

Pink *wadis* show in the dawn. Taza Haut brooded on a hill and, nearby, an amazing conglomeration of buildings called the Kasbah of Taourirt scowl at the train. Ouja is the border town, a dull but not unpleasant place of wide streets and solid European-style houses.

Rusty train wrecks lay beside the line to Oran. Tiemcen, however, shows a face of Andalusian elegance and Moorish arcades. Sidi-bel-Abbas smells of Foreign Legionnaires. The most Moorish-looking building in Oran is the chaotic railway station, where a corner seat on the train may be won by starting a rumour that it is to arrive at an adjacent platform.

INFORMATION BOX

Termini	Casablanca and Gabes
Countries	Morocco to Tunisia
Distance	1,778 km (1,105 miles)
Construction began	1915

● ABOVE
The Casablanca to Tangier express waits at Sidi Slimane.

● LEFT
The through diesel express of Moroccan Railways on its way from Marrakesh to Tangier via Casablanca and Rabat.

As in many industrial countries, the railway route into the capital is not the most attractive. The line sneaks in by the back door through the dingiest of industrial complexes. Onwards to Constantine and its amazing rock formations and a deep ravine traversed by slender bridges. The next main station is Annaba – once known as Bône. The trains that creep out of Annaba are equipped with third-class coaches, which are fit only for the knacker's (junk) yard, several compartments being both windowless and seatless. Souk-Ahras is the border town, some 16 km (10 miles) from the Tunisian frontier. Here, on the fringe of war, the border police sport brigand-style uniforms and swaggers.

In Tunisia, however, things change dramatically and abruptly. The trains are reasonably clean and in better order, even though the general feeling is that foreign tourists are not expected to use such lowly vehicles. On the train to Tunis, the customs officers have the habit of searching bags by the simple expedient of turning them upside down.

The 190 km (118 miles) of line between the border and the capital is narrow – metre-gauge – which explains the change of train. Though a fraction of the size of its massive neighbour, Tunisia can boast a track mileage of 2,200 against Algeria's 2,570.

In the south of the country, at Sfax, one has to change trains again. However, the onward connection to Gabes is poor, and the trains that eventually arrive seem as reluctant as the traveller is eager to reach the end of the line.

● **ABOVE**
A modern passenger train passes Bab Tisera (Sidi Kacem) *en route* from Casablanca to Fez.

● **RIGHT**
A passenger train arrives at Rabat.

Cairo to Aswan
The Star of Egypt

Although the all-sleeper express has lost its name today, tourism up the River Nile is 120 years old. Thomas Cook & Son (more particularly his son John) organized tourist river steamers on the Nile from about the mid-1870s. They were based in Cairo, which was connected with Egypt's main port Alexandria by the first railway in the Middle East, built in 1855. It included a bridge over the Nile outside Cairo, also used by the Star of Egypt on leaving Cairo Main. Wagons-Lits, creators of the Orient Express, celebrated their Silver Jubilee in 1898 by expanding simultaneously into Russia and Egypt.

Here the cars were painted white to reflect heat and had double roofs, while dining cars, built by Ringhoffer in Prague, had primitive air-conditioning, with blocks of ice cooling the air circulating between the skins of the roof. The great rival of Cook, whom they bought up in 1928, but lost during World War II, Wagons-Lits started sleepers with a diner in 1898 from Cairo to Luxor. At least until 1908, the lines which ran on up the Nile to Aswan remained narrow-gauge. The 1908 night train left Cairo on Mondays, Wednesdays and Saturdays, returning from Luxor on Tuesdays, Thursdays and Sundays.

The line leaves Cairo, crosses the Nile on the Alexandria line bridge and then turns upstream along the Nile's left bank through Assyut. It crosses the Nile at Nag Hamadi, and thereafter follows the right bank to Luxor and on to Aswan.

In 1906 Lord Dalziel bought from the executors of George Mortimer Pullman their British operations together with the exclusive rights to the name Pullman on railway cars throughout Europe and

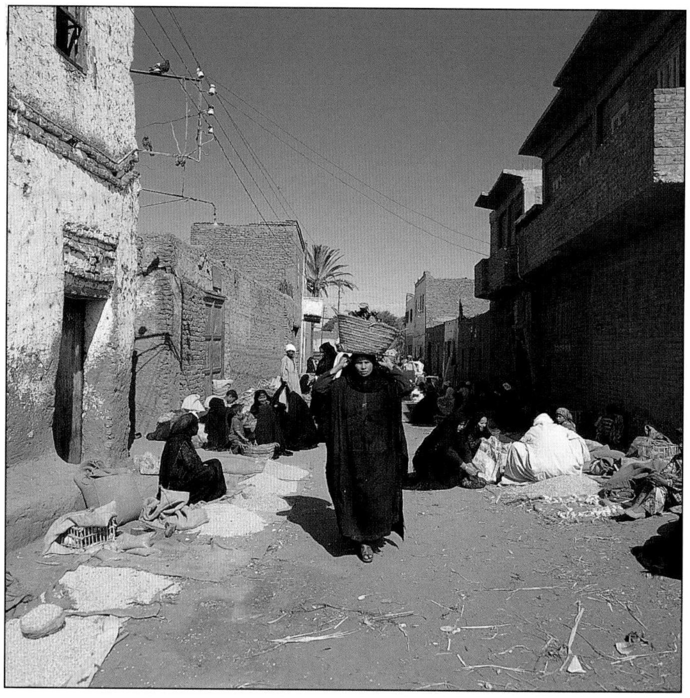

● RIGHT
A typical village market, or souk, of which many are seen on the journey.

● BELOW
Part of the frieze on the Thomas Cook office building in Leicester, depicting Cook's first full Egyptian tour begun in 1884.

● BELOW
An Egyptian Railways 1,500hp Bo-Bo waits to take its carriages to pick up Cairo-bound passengers at Aswan.

● LEFT
A French-built turbo train on the Cairo to Alexandria run in Egypt.

Egypt. Lord Dalziel gave these rights to Wagon-Lits, of which he was a director, in 1907. Wagons-Lits started using Pullmans in about 1925 and those for Egypt were shipped, newly built, direct from England. Lord Dalziel died in 1928, a few weeks after Wagons-Lits had swallowed up Cook, in the pretence that it was a merger.

Further Pullman cars were sent out in 1929, when the Sunshine Express, an all-Pullman day train from Cairo to Luxor, was started. New sleeping cars now ran in the night train, named Star of Egypt. At Aswan it continued to El Shallal, above the cataracts and the Aswan Dam, connecting with steamers to Wadi Halfa, in the Sudan, where the Sudanese Railways line to Khartoum avoids a big bend in the river. When the new Aswan Dam was built, the Aswan terminus was forced to move to El Sadd el Ali.

INFORMATION BOX

The Star of Egypt	
Termini	Cairo and Aswan
Country	Egypt
Distance	960 km (597 miles)
Date of opening	1908

● ABOVE
A mechanized maintenance train in Egypt.

The Sunshine Pullman ended its life in 1939, but the sleeping cars were revived after the war, and the Star of Egypt continued until around 1958-9 when Wagons-Lits was sequestered. The Egyptians found they could not really manage without them, and the Egyptian Republic Railways allowed them back, setting up a joint company to run the train. The Hungarian sleeping cars that ERR had bought were relegated to slow trains, and the modern-day all-sleeper train, with lounge car, now has German vehicles built in the 1980s by Messerschmidt MBB. A supply car replaces the diner, and meals are served in the cabins.

At present one train suffices on the route – most people either cruise on the Nile or fly. Thomas Cook still run the Nile cruise ships, but mostly these belong to other companies. Now the journey by all-sleeper train, which terminates at Aswan, takes some 16 hours – the 1938 journey was half an hour faster.

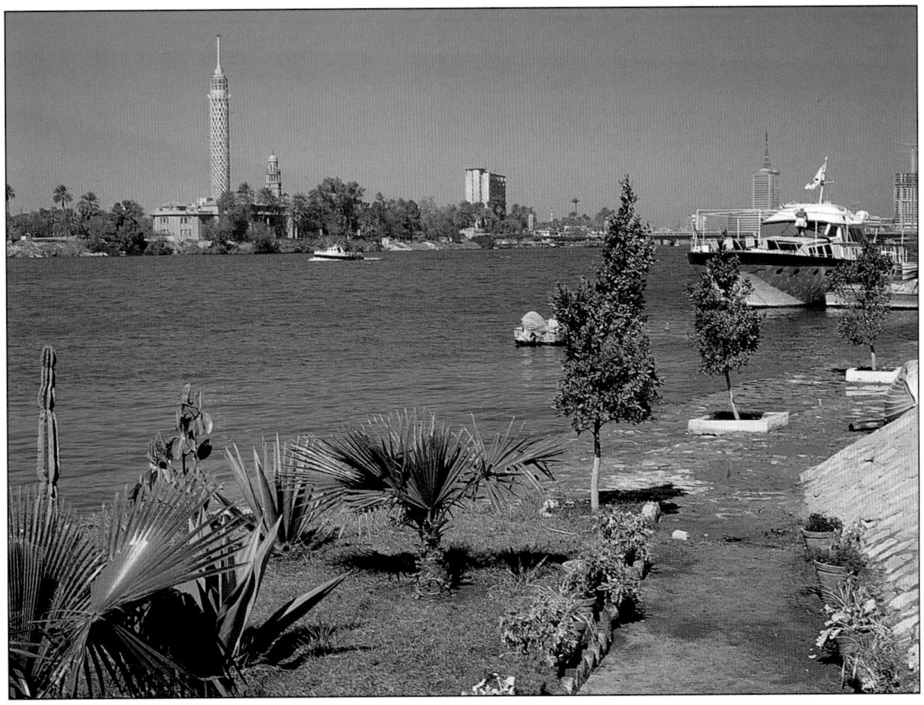

● BELOW
For much of the journey, the train travels by the Nile, seen here near Cairo.

Nairobi to Kampala

When construction of the then East African Railway began in 1898, it appeared to be going "from nowhere through nowhere to nowhere", and so they called it the "Lunatic Line". But there was a purpose. The aim, besides building a railway line through unknown East Africa to the once remote inland country of Uganda, was to help put down the detested Arab slave trade.

Victorian crusading enterprise in East Africa was chiefly directed at Uganda. Kenya was an afterthought. The crusade needed a railway so, with the matter-of-fact approach characteristic of the times, a railway was driven all the way from Mombasa on the Indian Ocean. If the track had to rise many metres up and down again, what did it matter? So it was successfully driven across hundreds of kilometres of bush alive with marauding wild animals, disease-carrying swamps and the lunar trough of the Great Rift itself, to Lake Victoria.

The line reached Kisumu after unbelievable feats of human endurance and engineering, and was later pushed forward to Kampala and beyond. From the coast, the line snaked through the uplands, infested by lions that killed some 200 construction workers, to reach a well in the deserted Kikuyu country. It came to the great Rift Valley escarpment, down which trains had to be lowered on an inclined plane assisted by rope haulage, and then continued over the Mau Summit to Kisumu on the shores of Lake Victoria. Here a prefabricated ship was launched, and Kampala, capital of Uganda, became accessible to the outside world via a journey of under five days. Nowhere else in the world, and at no time in history, has a journey been so dramatically shortened from six months'

ABOVE
Locomotive No. 5932 "Ol' Donya Sabuk" seen here hauling a Mombasa to Nairobi freight at Athi River.

INFORMATION BOX

Termini	Nairobi and Kampala
Countries	Kenya and Uganda
Length	1,338 km (831 miles)
Date construction commenced	1898

ABOVE
Derailed on the soggy Kasese Extentions, this locomotive was back in service within three months.

LEFT
A train approaches Jinja bridge near the Ripon Falls, the source of the Nile.

● **RIGHT**
An East African Railways Class 59 4-8-2+4-8-2 Mountain Class Garratt pulls heavily away from Voi at the edge of the Tsavo game reserve in Kenya with a heavy freight from Mombasa, bound for the Kenyan capital, Nairobi.

dangerous walking to a four-day ride in what was then comparative comfort. At the same time, the line opened up both Uganda and Kenya and was instrumental in the development of East Africa's major metropolis, Nairobi.

By early 1997 all rail services except a once-weekly international one terminated at the Kenya-Uganda border, but on this particular journey, 20 years or so earlier, the train was the last non-intercontinental through service to operate for some time. A military crisis had arisen, and President Idi Amin's army was poised to invade Kenya.

Deciding to press on regardless, the journey had to be confined. The train out of Nairobi was a lesser animal than that of the Mombassa-Nairobi Express, but adequate enough. And when one has the stupendous sight of the Rift valley *en route*, a reasonably clean and openable window is all that you really require.

On the floor of the Rift valley lies the town of Nakuru and, to the south of it, Lake Nakaru, an expanse of shallow, saline water, the shores of which are the sacred nesting ground of over 10,000 flamingos.

Unfortunately, the train was kept standing at the Kenyan border station of Malaba for five hours, following which it drew into Tororo. Between these two points the train was virtually empty – a somewhat lonely experience in a potential war zone. But the coaches filled up at Tororo.

● **BELOW LEFT**
An East African Railways Class 59 4-8-2+2-8-4 Garratt locomotive, built by Beyer Peacock of Manchester in 1955, rounds the spiral that forms part of the steep climb up the coastal escarpment from Mombasa on the Indian Ocean.

Notwithstanding the many stops at the wayside stations, the train did its best to make up for lost time. Each station was a colourful pageant of people, though few seemingly had any business with the railway; it was just that the station was the community centre – the place where the action was. At Jinja we crossed the River Nile.

It was raining when we reached Kampala and, climbing the stairs towards the exit, I was intercepted by what I later learned was a plain-clothes agent of the security service. The ensuing developments form no part of this rail narrative but, briefly, entailed my being arrested as a likely spy (for showing an interest in the railway), my interrogation in Kampala's grizzly central police station and prison, which took place over several days and nights, and my final release.

I was put aboard (i.e. left clinging to the step of a packed coach of) the seemingly very last train allowed through to Nairobi, where I arrived none the worse for my ill-fated Kampala visit except for a deficiency of sleep and a good meal.

● **BELOW**
East African Railways Class 59 4-8-2+2-8-4 Garratt No. 5922 "Mount Blackett" climbs the steep coastal escarpment away from Mombasa with a Nairobi-bound freight.

CAPE TOWN TO PRETORIA

THE BLUE TRAIN

The first luxury train to run the 3 ft 6 in gauge route from Cape Town to Pretoria was started in 1903. This was operated by the Cape Government Railway and the Central South African Railway. In 1910, on the formation of the Union of South Africa, all the country's independent lines amalgamated to form South African Railways, and the train was named the Union Limited. Although the train was a luxury one-class express, which required supplementary fares, it was extremely popular, so much so that in the 1930s more coaches had to be added and the smart Pacifics, which were used to haul the train, were replaced with 4-8-2s.

The twice-weekly train was renamed the Blue Train (Bloutrein) in April 1939. It was, of course, not the first time a train had been so named, for the Train Bleu had been running from Paris to the Côte d'Azur since the 1920s. This change of name coincided with the introduction of new blue-and-cream carriages with clerestory roofs; the locomotives, however, continued to be in the black of South African Railways. The compartments were super deluxe,

● **LEFT**
The Blue Train at Johannesburg station.

● **BELOW LEFT**
A head-on view of the Blue Train.

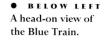

INFORMATION BOX

THE BLUE TRAIN	
Termini	Cape Town and Pretoria
Country	South Africa
Distance	1,607 km (999 miles)
Date of first run	1910

● **BELOW LEFT**
The Blue Train traversing the Hex River valley.

● **BELOW RIGHT**
The Blue Train is not without luxuries, such as facilities for a wash and brush up.

dust-proofed and air-conditioned with blue leather upholstered seats, loose cushions and writing tables with headed notepaper. At the rear of the train was an observation car. In spite of the 3 ft 6 in gauge the body width of these coaches was 3 m (10 ft).

Such was the popularity of the train that, in spite of the high prices, reservations had to be made far in advance. To provide room for the various on-board services, including fully equipped bathrooms, only 100 passengers could be catered for on each journey. The train was electrically hauled by blue locomotives between Pretoria and Kimberley, and again between Beaufort West and Cape Town, and scheduled to do three round trips weekly from October to March and one from April to September.

President Nelson Mandela inaugurated the "new" Blue Train in June 1997. Built from the undercarriage of the original Blue Train sets, these two new trains feature only two grades of on-board accommodation – luxury and deluxe – as opposed to the previous four.

The luxury suites differ from the deluxe in that they are more spacious and offer larger bathrooms – deluxe ones have private shower or bath, luxury ones all have baths. There is 24-hour butler service, laundry service and two lounge cars, and while all the suites are equipped with televisions and telephones, the luxury suites in addition have CD players and video recorders. There is also live footage on TV from a camera positioned in the front of the train, giving passengers a "driver's-eye" view of their journey.

With this impressive level of upgrading of the Blue Train, capacity on board has inevitably been reduced from 107 to 84. The Blue Train no longer serves Johannesburg, routing via Germiston instead as it travels between Pretoria and Cape Town. There are several departures throughout the year between Pretoria and Victoria Falls.

● **ABOVE**
The Blue Train running through the beautiful Hex River valley.

● **LEFT**
The Blue Train with the unmistakable Table Mountain in the background.

Cape Town to Victoria Falls

Railways in the Cape Colony date back to 1857, when a pioneering line was opened from Cape Town to Wellington – a 72 km (45 mile) journey. In 1873 the first trains completed the 1,036 km (644 miles) from Cape Town to Kimberley across the Karoo, and as Cecil Rhodes progressed through Africa, the iron road was laid northwards, the 235 km (146 mile) section from Kimberley to De Aar being laid in an impressive 20 months between March 1884 and November 1885. The route of the Pride of Africa is from Cape Town, via Beaufort West, De Aar, Kimberley, Klerksdorp, Johannesburg, Pretoria, Mafeking (border), Gaborone, Plumtree (border), Bulawayo, and Hwange to Victoria Falls.

The modern flat-roofed station at Cape Town seems an improbable place to embark on one of the world's most entrancing railway journeys, but on Platform 24 stands no ordinary train. Drawn up like guards on parade, the Pride of Africa, resplendent in bottle-green livery, evokes the sublimity of a truly grand occasion. At the head of the train, a pair of Class 6E1 3,000V DC Bo-Bo electrics, in the rather old-fashioned rusty-brown colours of South African Railways, look purposeful and

• LEFT
The observation car of the Pride of Africa allows unimpeded views across the African bush. Comfortable armchairs make this an ideal venue to watch the passing scenery, while the open platform gives photographers superb views of the passing landscapes.

INFORMATION BOX

Termini	Cape Town and Victoria Falls
Countries	South Africa to Zimbabwe
Distance	3,200 km (2,000 miles)
Date of completion of first section	1873

• LEFT
A double-headed train crosses over the Kaaiman River bridge.

● BELOW
Locomotive No. 519 returning from the cement works at Gwanda, Zimbabwe.

● BOTTOM RIGHT
An impressive line-up of Garratts at Bulawayo shed.

● BELOW
Rovos Rail owns four steam locomotives. No. 439, Tiffany, is the oldest, built in 1893 and restored by Dunns Locomotive more than 90 years later. Numbers 2701, 2702 and 3360 are all Class 19D locomotives.

ready to haul their charge over the 708 km (440 miles) to Beaufort West, from just over sea level at Cape Town to over 1,219 m (4,000 ft) across the Karoo.

The dignified welcome for the passengers is in stark contrast to the local Metro trains busily heading off into the suburbs, their human cargoes packed tighter than sardines. Rohan Vos, owner and visionary behind the Pride of Africa, is often on hand to give a few handy hints on how to get the most out of the pan-African odyssey, before he bids the train farewell, toasting the travellers with fine South African sparkling wine.

Nestling beneath the distinctively flat-topped massif of Table Mountain, Cape Town enjoys one of the most spectacular settings on earth. As the Pride of Africa begins its journey northwards, it soon leaves the compact patchwork of red- and white-roofed houses and modern office blocks behind as the tracks follow the mighty circle of Table Bay with its encircling ocean before heading inland.

In the wine country of Paarl and the Hex River valley, tangled vines grow in the foothills of starkly chiselled mountains. These are modest farmsteads, their white porticoes guarded by cypresses at the end of rutted dirt roads. Here and there, roosting in the scrub, ostriches preen their feathers among indifferent sheep and horses.

Africa has been a magnet for adventurers ever since Xenophon's men took time out to hunt the wild ostrich, and in our own times Rohan Vos has single-handedly created one of southern Africa's most romantic travelling idylls. Rovos Rail is his dreamchild, and in 1986 he started lovingly restoring ancient, abandoned railway coaches and proud steam locomotives.

Dating from 1919, each sleeping car, observation car, bar and lounge car, as well as the atmospheric Victorian and Edwardian dining cars, combines the opulence of pre-war style with subtle modern innovations. Sleeping accommodation is in suites with double or twin beds, together with private showers and toilets.

As the sun all but disappears, leaving a last explosion of light along the earth's rim, the train arrives at Matjiesfontein. Here an hour-long visit can be made to the historical hamlet where, over one hundred years ago, Laird Logan set up a small refreshment hotel to revictual the hungry and thirsty travellers of the Cape Government Railways. The graceful

● **RIGHT**
A painting of The
Royal Train in
Rhodesia.

● **BELOW LEFT**
A Class 15 Garratt
storms past near
Thomson Junction,
Zimbabwe.

● **BELOW
RIGHT**
A Class 20 just north
of Thomson
Junction *en route* to
Victoria Falls.

hotel, named after Lord Milner, provides
an opportunity to take the evening air
and enjoy a small draught of the famous
Castle beer.

As the train continues its journey, the
Karoo's horizon becomes scarlet, the sky
salmon, the earth blood – it is the
drunken dusk of the desert. Passengers
become ensconced in the observation
car, aperitif in hand, watching the African
night creep up on the train.

Coach No. 148, Pafuri, was originally
built in 1911 as an A-17 type dining car
comprising a small bar, a 24-seat dining
section, and a kitchen. In 1924, she was
converted into a full 46-seater,
responding to an increasing percentage of

passengers taking meals on the great
trains of Africa, such as the Diamond
Express, the Imperial Mail and the
African Express.

Today's passengers enjoy evoking
the nostalgia of the great days of travel
in this most romantic of settings,
surrounded by seven pairs of carved
roof-supporting pillars and arches. Later,
the travellers fall asleep to the rhythmical,
hypnotic motion of the train's wheels.
Despite the narrow 3 ft 6 in gauge of
South Africa's railways, the ride is
surprisingly smooth.

Unnoticed at Beaufort West the
current changes to a.c., and now two
Class 7E Co-Co locomotives are attached

to haul the train to De Aar. During the
night, the 235 km (146 mile) stretch of
non-electrified line from De Aar to
Kimberley is reached, and a pair of Class
34 Co-Co diesel electrics put in charge.

The following day sees the train arrive
at the fine old Victorian station of
Kimberley. This city of diamonds is set in
the flat, austere landscape of the Karoo.
History is rekindled as lunch is enjoyed
in the famous Kimberley Club, wistfully
recapturing the spirit of the reign of
Rhodes and Jameson, who clinched so
many deals on these premises. Now with
two powerful, high-speed 3,000V d.c.
Bo-Bo Class 12Es in command, the Pride
of Africa speeds towards Pretoria.

The following day, after a sightseeing
tour of Pretoria, the 17-carriage train
heads north through groves of orange,
papaya and avocado, past depressing
townships where flocks of children run
down to the tracks smiling and waving. In
the observation and lounge cars the railborne safari begins in earnest as sightings
of impala, kudu and zebra give us a
foretaste of this unforgettable close
encounter with Africa.

Crossing into Botswana at Mafeking
the Pride of Africa undergoes one of a
series of no fewer than seven locomotive
changes between Pretoria and Victoria

● LEFT
A Zimbabwe train, headed by a maroon-liveried Garratt, poses on Victoria Falls bridge for this aerial photograph.

● BELOW
The spectacular bridge, just north of Victoria Falls, is a train photographer's dream. Once a year when the Pride of Africa makes its momentous Edwardian Safari journey from Cape Town to Dar es Salaam, it crosses this mighty bridge. The end of the train is close to the Zimbabwe border just north of Victoria Falls station, the front close by the Zambian border a few miles to the south of Livingston.

Falls. The mood on board is one of anticipation as passengers savour Cape crayfish and Karoo lamb washed down with Chardonnays and Cabernets.

The steepest gradient encountered is 1:50, as the train makes its assault on the steep-sided mountains that separate the lush, fertile Hex River valley and the elevated, arid Karoo. The climb of 533 m (1,750 ft) over 82 km (51 miles) is the most spectacular section of the journey; its highest point lies just south of Johannesburg at 1,834 m (6,017 ft). The series of four tunnels in the 16.4 km (10.2 mile) long Hex River tunnel system are ranked as the fourth largest in the world and are by far the single most outstanding feature of the journey between Cape Town and Victoria Falls. The tunnels are dead straight, and the longest of them, the northernmost, is spectacular when viewed from the observation car – you can still see the entrance as you leave the exit.

The last complete day on the train is filled with spectacular views of the African bush. After crossing into Zimbabwe at Plumtree, an afternoon visit is made to Bulawayo. Home to Lobengula, King of the Matabele nation in 1870, the city went on to become synonymous with mining. Here a Class 15 Garratt articulated steam locomotive takes charge. This huge 28-wheeler hauls the Pride of Africa through the night along one of the longest stretches of straight railway line in the world – the 116 km (72 miles) between Gwaai and Dete on the eastern edge of the Hwange National Park. Musi-oa-tunya ("smoke that thunders") – the African name for the Victoria Falls – heralds journey's end. The screaming of the wheels as the train rounds the final curve adds to the dramatic sense of theatre that this 3,218 km (2,000 mile) pan-African adventure has created. Truly, the Pride of Africa is an iconoclast, following in the footsteps of empire.

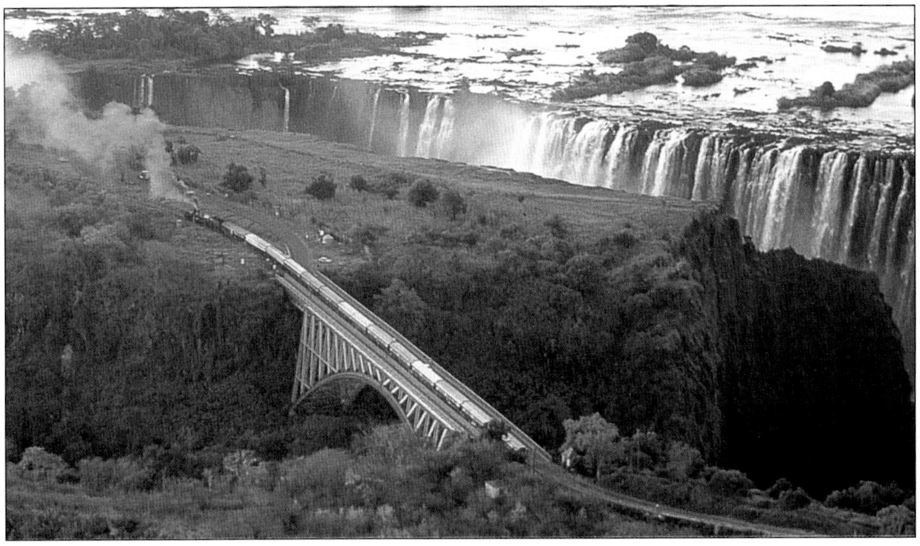

CAPE TOWN TO PRETORIA
THE TRANS KAROO

The Trans Karoo is named after its crossing of the Karoo Desert, which covers around one third of South Africa, and is larger than Great Britain and Ireland. Although the Karoo is not of the sand dune type, it proved to be a difficult barrier to cross. Another kind of barrier is the altitude of the Highveld on which Johannesburg is situated; the city is over 1,524 m (5,000 ft) above sea level. The combination of these two factors continues to make operation of trains between these principal towns of the Republic of South Africa (RSA) a continuing challenge, even after electrification of the line.

The lack of water in the desert led to the introduction of a feature unique to South Africa, the condensing tender. These elongated vehicles contained steam-condensing equipment and were used with many Class 25 steam locomotives to reduce water consumption by recycling as much steam as possible. The result was that the British-built locomotives could travel over 1,100 km (700 miles) on one tender of water.

Modernization has shortened the Cape Town to Pretoria journey from the 30 hours taken in 1978, and the Trans Karoo now runs daily rather than five days a week as it did then. However, a second train over the route, running to a schedule 12 hours later on four days a week, has been deleted. The reduction in passenger rail travel has been repeated across the country and is well illustrated by the long lines of stored passenger-coaches outside Cape Town.

The Trans Karoo runs daily between Cape Town and Pretoria via De Aar, Kimberley and Johannesburg, taking 26 hours for the 1,600 km (1,000 mile) journey. The famous Blue Train continues to operate over the same route three days per week, but is now aimed at the luxury travel and tourist market, whereas the Trans Karoo operates the "genuine" passenger service.

The Trans Karoo departs the large Cape Town terminus station from platform 24, which is reserved for this and the few other long-distance services.

● **BELOW**
Cape wine area farms near Paarl, seen from the Trans Karoo.

● **RIGHT**
SAR Class 6E electric locomotive No. E1184 outside Beaufort West depot sporting the latest Spoornet livery. These 3,340 hp locomotives were built in 1970–1 by Union Carriage and Wagon Co. (UCW), at Nigel, Transvaal, with equipment from AEI in Manchester, England. Double-headed members of this class haul the Trans Karoo from Cape Town to Beaufort West and from De Aar to Pretoria.

● **BELOW**
The SAR steam locomotive dump at Millsite. The large locomotive in the centre of the picture is one of the large Bayer-Garratt articulated locomotives.

INFORMATION BOX

THE TRANS KAROO

Termini	Cape Town and Pretoria
Country	South Africa
Distance	1,600 km (1,000 miles)
Commencement of building	1892

● **OPPOSITE BELOW**
A steam-hauled Trans Karoo passing Millsite. The locomotives are 4-8-4s of class 25NC, Nos. 3476 and 3404. These locomotives were constructed in 1953–4 by North British in Glasgow, Scotland, and Henschel of Kassel, Germany.

The train the author travelled in was made up of 15 coaches, a car-carrying van, a steam-heating van and two electric locomotives of Class 6E. The weather was cool enough for wisps of steam to be seen emanating from the steam-heating van. The locomotives would be changed a couple of times *en route*, at Beaufort West and De Aar. A Class 7E was used between these points as this route is electrified at a different voltage, 25kV a.c. as opposed to 3,000V d.c. from Cape Town and into Pretoria. The Friday departure from Pretoria as far as Klerksdorp, and the Saturday return, were steam hauled using double-headed 4-8-4s of Class 25NC.

First impressions of the train are not helped by the tatty appearance of the paintwork, which belies the state of the interior. Inside, the coaches are clean and simply but effectively furnished. The train was formed with three classes of accommodation. The first and second class were sleeper coaches marshalled each side of the restaurant cars. The third class, mainly day coaches, was separated from the rest of the train by a door that remained firmly locked throughout the trip. There are on-board showers located at the end of each sleeping coach.

● **BELOW**
The Karoo near Beaufort West. The background hills are of a shape common in the desert.

The restaurant car (actually two coaches, one containing the kitchen and staff quarters, the other the seating area) provides good food, although the approach to service seems to be of the same vintage as the coaches. In addition, there is a very effective trolley service of drinks and snacks. The train crew, who were on duty for the entire journey, included an armed guard. This is not so much due to the high crime levels as to control drunken passengers.

The train first heads through the Cape Town suburbs and then into the Cape wine areas of Stellenbosch and Paarl. This area is characterized not only by the vineyards, but also by the famous white-painted, Dutch-style farmhouses. Of particular note is Huguenot Station in an area named after the early French settlers. This is built in the Cape Dutch style, but it has very British influences in the footbridge and signals. The Cape wine area is within the Cape Town electrified suburban rail network, which is served by brightly coloured suburban EMUs.

After initially travelling north, the train turns in a north-westerly direction, which is the wrong way for Johannesburg, and it is this diversion to find a crossing-point in the coastal mountains that makes competition with road transport so difficult. After Herman, the line curves towards the mountains and follows a winding pass before descending into the Breede valley. This is an area of farmlands and orchards; a very English-looking landscape, except for the shapes of the distant hills.

After De Doorn, four hours out of Cape Town, a couple of very lengthy tunnels take the train to the start of the Karoo. One of the first things to notice is

● ABOVE
SAR coaches at Pretoria. The blue-and-grey Interpax coaches are of the type used on the Trans Karoo.

● BOTTOM
Typical Karoo scenery between Touwsrivier and Matjiesfontein.

● BELOW
An SAR electric locomotive of Class 7E on a freight train at Beaufort West. These 4,340 hp locomotives were built by UCW and the "50 Cycles Group" (a consortium of European electrical equipment manufacturers) in 1978–9. This class hauls the Trans Karoo between Beaufort West and De Aar.

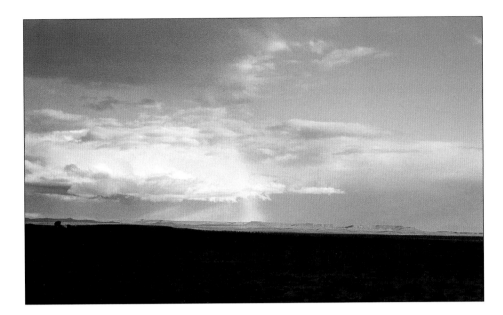

● LEFT
View of the Karoo and rainbow, north of Prince Albert Road.

an ostrich farm complete with a rail-connected loading dock. Another is the sturdy shrubs covering the desert. These have varied flower colours, and their density thins out as the train gets farther into the Karoo. The only "wildlife" visible from the train are some very hardy sheep. The other dominating features are the interesting shapes of the hills, which tend to be flat-topped and sheer-sided with a surface of shattered rock and no significant vegetation.

Two lasting memories of crossing the desert are worth recording. After travelling through a rare rain shower, there was a magnificent rainbow against the darkened sky and the strangely shaped hills. Secondly, a stop at a passing loop in the middle of the night. Not only was the air very cold, but the author has never seen a night sky so clear and starry, and with no man-made light visible from the horizons.

While the very necessary inclusion of the heating van was unusual in October, not everyone seemed aware of the arrangement. The van was taken off the train at Beaufort West. After this, the train became exceedingly cold in the desert night, not properly warming up until the sun was well up.

The few trains that passed us on this Sunday were all containerized freights. It was clear that most sidings at local stations were out of use, as road traffic has taken over the local and short-haul freight, leaving only the long-haul and large-volume freight to the railways. However, much of the route showed signs of modernization, as curves and gradients had been eased, and new tunnels built to avoid difficult sections of the route, indicating that the railway does have a future.

The Johannesburg end of the journey is dominated first by farm land, and then by the mining industry, with many spoil heaps visible until you are almost into the city. One site worth looking out for is at Millsite, a few minutes before arrival at Krugersdorp. Adjacent to the SAR locomotive depot is the main store of withdrawn and stored steam locomotives.

The morning run through the Johannesburg suburbs showed a stark contrast with Cape Town. Nearly every house has high railings, usually with razor wire, and several stations have guards armed with shotguns.

The train proceeds from Johannesburg, to end its journey at the imposing Pretoria station. Opposite stands the Victoria Hotel, now owned by luxury train operator Rovos Rail. This is a traditional colonial-style hotel, in contrast to the buildings around it. Rovos Rail also operates between Cape Town and Johannesburg, but its service is even more expensive than the Blue Train.

● BELOW
SAR suburban EMUs, including No. 13150, in Cape Town carriage sidings, showing the old and new liveries. The yellow livery is branded "Metro". No. 13150, of Class 5M2A, was built by UCW in the 1960s, one of a type that was constructed by two builders between 1958 and 1985. The mountain in the background is Devil's Peak, with Table Mountain behind and to the right.

ISTANBUL TO BAGHDAD
THE TAURUS EXPRESS

Started in 1930, the Taurus Express (Toros Ekspresi in Turkish) linked London to Cairo and Berlin to Baghdad. Only the English Channel and the Bosporus needed ferries. With Germans in charge of operations, it followed the route of the Baghdad Railway, a Turkish enterprise that had been funded with money from the Deutsche Bank. Once controlled by the French, the Baghdad Railway was taken over in 1880 by the British and in 1888 by Turkey.

From Istanbul the Ottoman Anatolian Railway retained its French title, handing over to the Baghdad Railway at Konya, an Islamic centre famous for the Mevlevi Order of Whirling Dervishes. Like Rome or Canterbury, the city has a holy atmosphere.

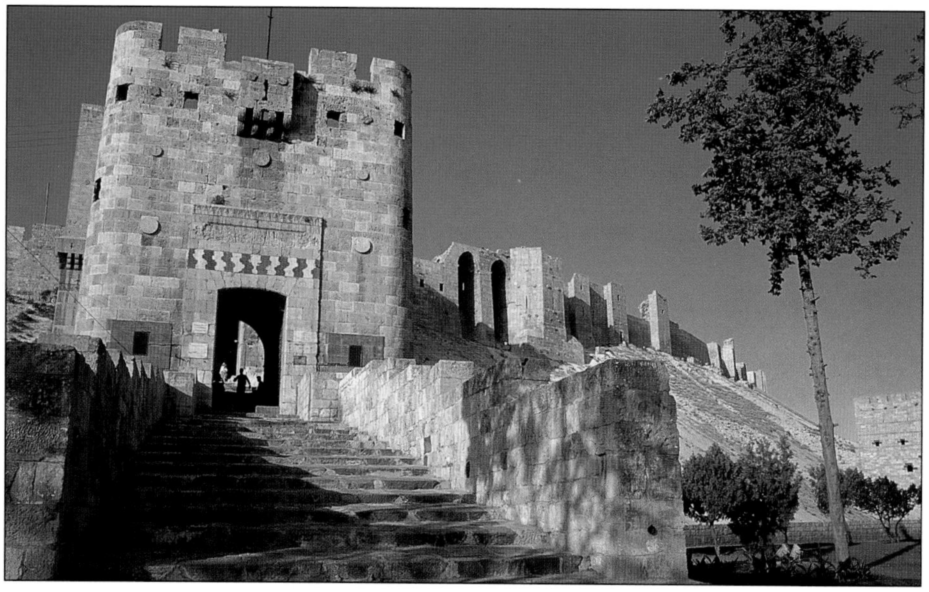

● **ABOVE RIGHT**
The imposing walls of the Citadel at Aleppo.

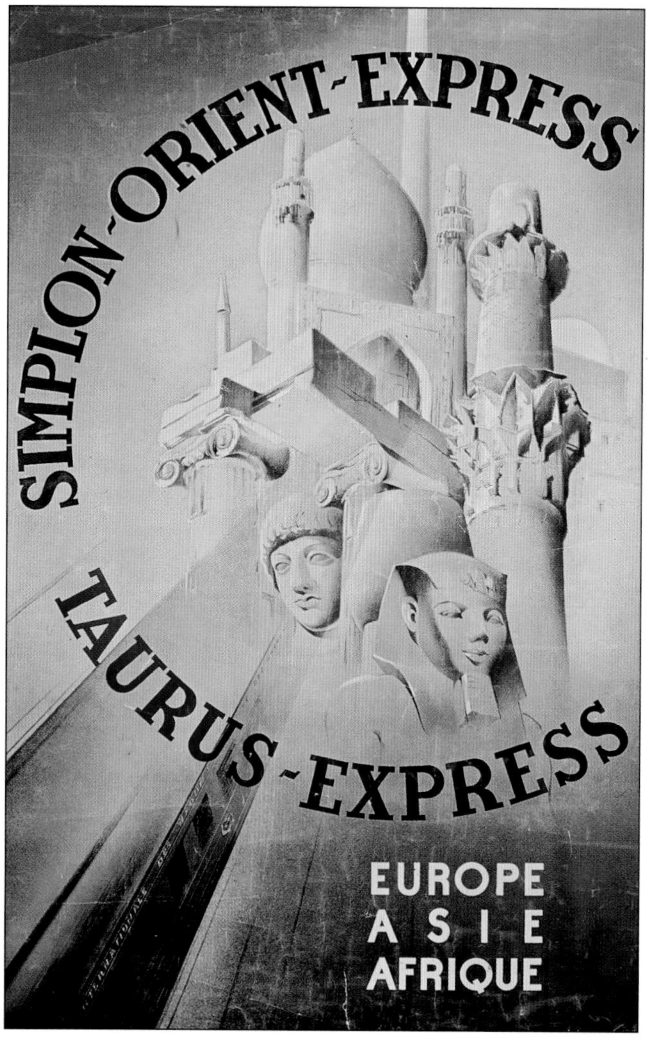

● **RIGHT**
Poster of the Simplon-Orient Express for the inauguration of the Taurus Express route via Ankara in 1930.

In the south of Turkey, the railway ran through the rich Cilician Plain that feeds most of the otherwise rocky desert with its patches of civilization. It was opened from Adana to Mersin via Yenice in 1886, but was taken over by the Deutsche Bank in 1906.

The CFOA started originally as a narrow-gauge line in 1873, along the north coast of the Marmora Sea and across the Ak Ova plain. After Arifiye, 36 m (118 ft) up, the line climbed through the Baleban gorge, then across

INFORMATION BOX

THE TAURUS EXPRESS	
Termini	Istanbul and Baghdad
Countries	Turkey and Iraq
Distance	2,566 km (1,595 miles)
Date building commenced	1893

FAR LEFT
The first Wagons-Lits sleepers in Asiatic Turkey, seen here on the Anatolia Express in 1927. These cars were put into service on the Taurus Express in 1930.

LEFT
An SG type sleeping-car compartment, built in Birmingham, England, for the Taurus Express. A feature of the compartment are the holders for fob watches.

the smallish Akhisar plain where tobacco, corn and mulberries grew. It then ascends 294 m (965 ft) through a narrow gorge, whose walls are about 90 m (300 ft) above the railway, to Bilecik, a steam-lovers' paradise. Here worked western Turkey's last huge steam banking 2-10-2 tank-engines, which hauled trains 16 km (10 miles) up another 390 m (1,280 ft) at a 1:40 gradient to Eskesehir on the Central plateau.

From Eskesehir, where Turkey's main railway works is situated, a branch line turned east to Angora (famous for its wool), which was reached by rail in 1892. The city was renamed Ankara in 1921 by Attaturk, when he made it his nation's capital. The British ambassador, not wanting to relocate to Ankara, hired some sleeping cars and a diner from Wagons-Lits and lived in them during the week, returning to his palatial Istanbul Embassy at the weekends.

In 1927 Wagons-Lits created the Anatolia Express, which went as far as Ankara, the Russians not wanting German-influenced railways extending too far eastward. In 1895, influenced by Germany's *Drang nach Osten*, a railway to connect Konya and Baghdad was started simultaneously from both termini. By the time World War I broke out, the line had reached Samora (now in Iraq), 290 km (180 miles) south of Monsul and 121 km (75 miles) from Baghdad.

ABOVE
Only two all-Wagons-Lits trains existed after the war: the Train Bleu in France and the Ankara Express in Turkey. The latter, hauled by a Henschel 2-8-2, is seen here arriving at Istanbul in 1957.

BELOW
A view of the city of Aleppo, stretching out, taken from the walls of the Citadel.

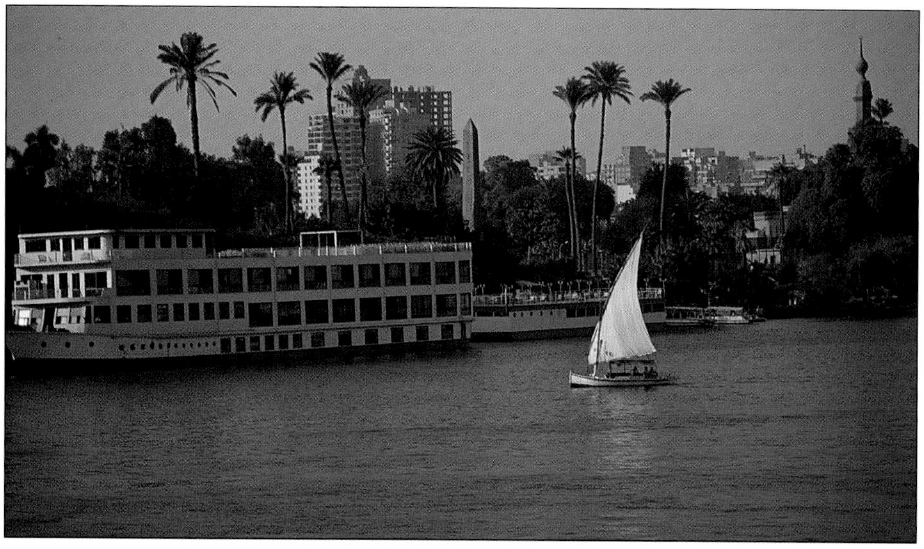

● ABOVE
A visit to Egypt is not complete without a cruise. Here we see a cruise ship and a felluca on the Nile at Cairo.

From Konya the line crossed the 64 km (40 mile) long Konya plain, followed by the Karaman plain to Cakmak, where it climbed from 61 m (200 ft) to 366 m (1,201 ft) in 29 km (18 miles), mostly at 1:40. The summit was at Kardesgedigi, where the 1935-built line from Ankara was joined. Thereafter the Taurus Express ran by Ankara, and Konya was only a secondary route.

Now, as the train began its great drop through the Cilician Gates to Yenice, from 1,468 m (4,816 ft) to 34 m (112 ft) in 105 km (65 miles), the Taurus mountains were on all sides. Pozanti, the only town for miles around, is 32 km (20 miles) from the top. From Andna, the Germans decided that the flat line on the coastal plain through Antioch would be too close to the sea (fearing seizure by the British), so they took an inland route from the Cilician Plain. This climbed back up to 732 m (2,402 ft), where they built the 1,495 m (4,905 ft) long Amanus tunnel, which took the train to Fevsipasa. Here the Taurus Express turned south through Meydan Ekbez to Aleppo. From Aleppo the line ran on towards Tripoli, which was the main supply line to Palestine.

In 1927, Attaturk formed the Turkish State railways, which, in 1919, took over from the French from Pozanti to Favaipasa. The French formed two companies – the Cenup, or Turkish Southern, and the Syrian-Baghdad lines. Both were worked and run by the same management between Aleppo and Tel Kotchek, 76 km (47 miles) beyond the Syrian frontier at Nusaybin. Until 1939, travellers to Baghdad left the train at Tel Kotchek, now El Yaroubish, which had a Wagons-Lits rest house, and motored to Kirkuk, the terminus of the narrow-gauge line to Baghdad. The Baghdad Railway was extended to Sanora in 1940. After 1940 the Taurus Express became a through train with sleepers and a diner, for the 2,566 km (1,595 miles) from Istanbul to Baghdad. This service ended in 1966.

Before World War II the Taurus ran three days a week to Tel Kotchek and three days a week to Tripoli, with a connecting sleeper from Aleppo on the days when the train ran to Tel Kotchek. At Tripoli the passengers transferred to Model A Ford motor cars. To avoid the heat they drove to Beirut early in the morning and rested for about four hours before going on to Haifa, avoiding the mountain barrier by driving along the beach – there was no road.

At Haifa, Wagons-Lits ran a sleeping car to Kantara East in Egypt, crossing from Palestine at Rafa, after passing

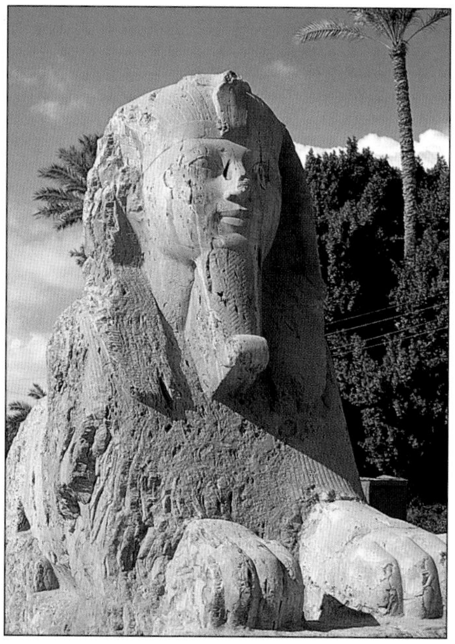

● ABOVE LEFT
The impressive Sphinx at Giza, just outside Cairo.

● LEFT
The Istanbul to Ankara express near Kaysari.

● LEFT
The Taurus Express near Bogazkopru.

Lydda Junction (for Jerusalem) and Gaza. The British-built Palestine Railways continued to run through to Kantara, where the pontoon bridge over the Suez Canal was removed for the benefit of larger liners. Passengers were ferried across to Kantara West, where Taurus passengers joined the last of the four daily trains of Egyptian State Railways, which had a Wagons-Lits Pullman running next to the dining car.

After Wagons-Lits withdrew in 1970, the Taurus Express continued to Baghdad, alternating with Haleb (Aleppo) or Gaziantep, where the dining car was removed.

The sleeping cars were accompanied by ordinary coaches, but today, because of the events of the Gulf War and continuing Kurdish troubles, the sleeping cars run only to Haleb or Gaziantep.

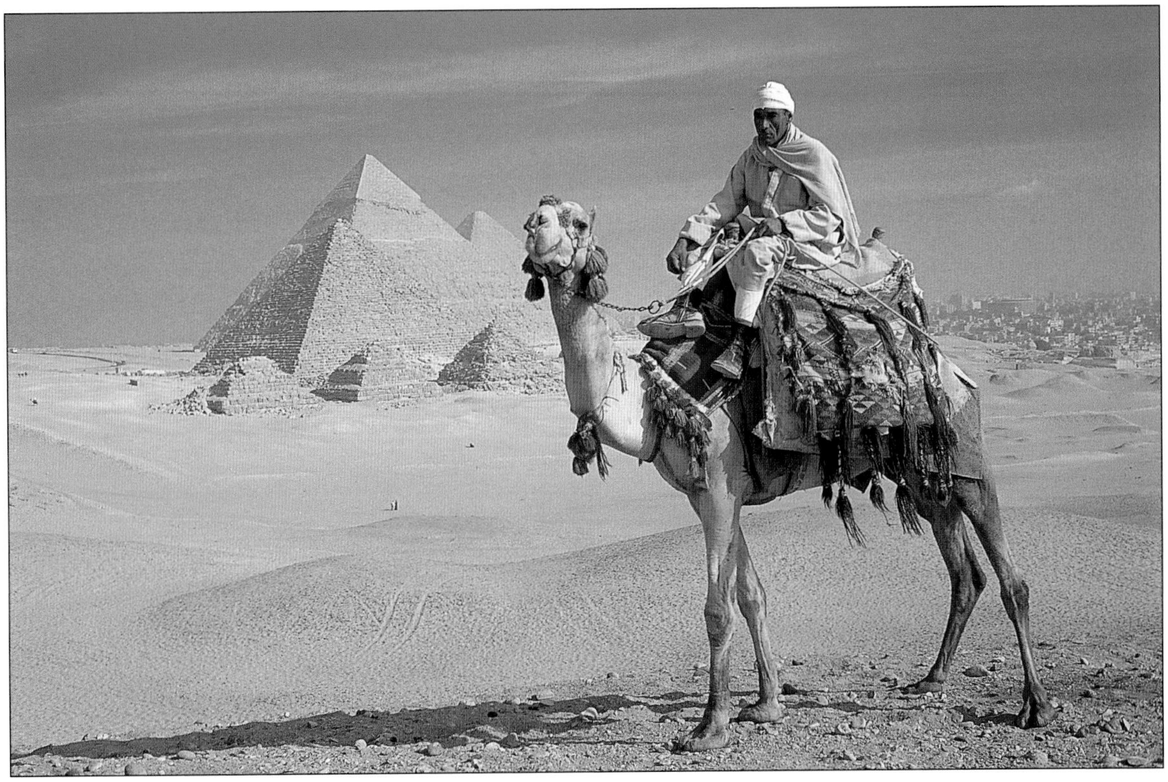

● RIGHT
One of the wonders of the ancient world, the pyramids at Giza are a romantic and evocative sign that the train is nearing Cairo, Egypt.

ISTANBUL TO KARS
THE DOGU EXPRESS

The Dogu Express, or Eastern Express in English, links Istanbul with Kars, the last town in Turkey before the Armenian frontier with Armenia.

Attaturk chose Ankara as his capital partly because it was the most easterly point of Turkey's railways when he came to power, and he immediately began extensions eastward. From Ankara, at an altitude of 876 m (2,874 ft), the line was continued for 300 km (186 miles) across the plateau before dropping 305 m (1,000 ft) at Pazali. There are a few tunnels to the Irmak River valley, a fertile area with poplar trees, maize, melons and sunflowers.

Running south-east, the line passes a munitions works before dividing at Bogazkopru, where the Taurus Express line to Adana turns south-west and the Dogu north-east. In 1935 the line reached Kayseri, some 378 km (235 miles) from Ankara.

The Dogu Express continues north-east to Sivas, 1,185 m (3,888 ft) above sea level, where the principal railway works for eastern Turkey are situated. The line, completed in 1936, continues from a junction shortly before Sivas, to Samsun on the Black Sea coast, where Attaturk mounted his attack on the Ottoman Empire in 1918.

From Sivas, the Dogu Express continues at more or less the same level, turning south-east and climbing over the foothills to reach the Upper Euphrates valley at Cetinkaya. The next section through the narrow Atma Gorge, an area prone to earthquakes, was not completed until 1967–8.

The resultant railway is a masterpiece of Turkish engineering with 13 tunnels in 50 km (31 miles) on the line to the plain at Erzincan. Near Eric, a village with a few cultivated fields and meagre fruit trees in a small plain liable to flooding, where the inhabitants perch somehow in

• BELOW
The Dogu Express near Eric.

• ABOVE
One of Turkey's most celebrated steam designs was the Skyliner 2-10-0. Of classic American appearance, these huge locomotives, which were built by the Vulcan Ironworks at Wilkes Barre between 1947 and 1949, were often to be seen hauling express trains.

• LEFT
A view of the city of Ankara taken from the walls of the Citadel.

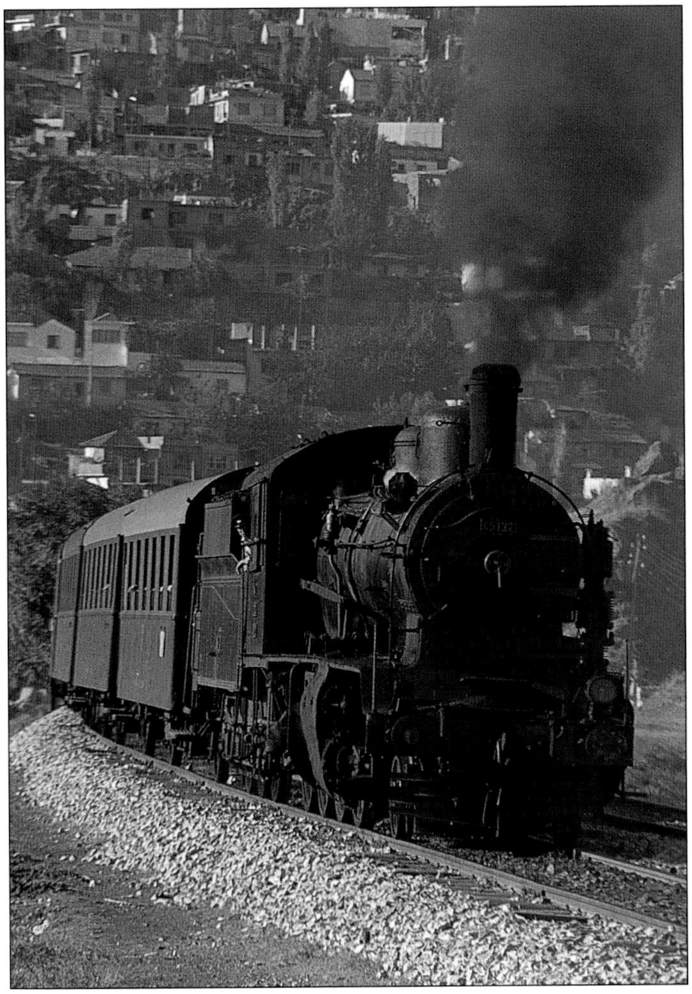

● LEFT
This Turkish State Railways 2-8-0 was built by Humbolt of Paris in 1912.

● BELOW
Another Skyliner 2-10-0 hauls a freight train in the mountains of northern Turkey.

INFORMATION BOX

THE DOGU EXPRESS	
Termini	Istanbul and Kars
Country	Turkey
Distance	1,944 km (1,208 miles)
Date of opening	1936

● BOTTOM
The Sultan Ahmet mosque in Istanbul.

primitive houses on the ledges on the gorge sides, there are 14 tunnels in 17 km (11 miles) of line.

In between the tunnels every kind of bridge is found crossing over the numerous clefts and tributaries that run into the Euphrates gorge. There are stone bridges, underslung-girder bridges, concrete and box-girder bridges – a *tour de force* as the precipices are so sheer as to be really frightening.

Finally the line drops down to Erzincan, 112 m (368 ft) above sea level. The Turks started building the line westward from Erzincan in 1937, but going east there are another 200 km (124 miles) across the plain to Erzerum, the capital of eastern Turkey, a line built in 1939. From here the train passes through more tunnels before emerging into the Araxes valley.

The Dogu follows the Araxes to Horasan before turning north, climbing to about 3,000 m (9,843 ft) and into the long Horasan tunnel.

The train then descends the fir-covered hills at a gradient of 1:40 to Sarikamis. The line from here to Kars was finished in Russian gauge in 1913 – just in time for World War I – and a narrow-gauge line was built from here to Erzerum in 1916. The Dogu ends its journey at Kars, usually arriving at the end of the day, in the gloomy dusk.

ISTANBUL TO TEHERAN
THE VAN GOLU EXPRESS

● BELOW
The eastbound Van Golu Express, east of Malatya station.

The Van Golu (Lake Van) Express was one of the last Turkish Railways routes to link the west and east of Turkey. The lake, 97 km (60 miles) across and 1,719 m (5,640 ft) above sea level, was far from the railway until 1964. The Van Golu takes the same route as the Dogu Express between Istanbul and Cetinkaya, and then follows the Euphrates to Malatya, which was earlier reached from Fevsipasa. In 1939 the line was extended to Elazig with an altitude of 1,000 m (3,280 ft). The difficult mountainous route from Elazig was not started until after World War II. It reached Genc in 1954 and Mus in 1955.

Ten years elapsed before the line was continued to Tatvan on Lake Van's western shore. The first part of the route follows the River Ningrad, which turns south-east and winds gently through the mountains to join the Tigris. More mountains block the way to Lake Van. The Van Golu terminated here on Tatvan Pier, 1,884 km (1,171 miles) from Istanbul. The Turkish State railway (TCDD) operates a train ferry that takes four hours to cross Lake Van. From Van, a new railway was started that ran another 160 km (100 miles) east to Kapikoy, on the frontier, and over the border to Razi in Iran.

The Iranians built this difficult line through the rocky, harsh, undulating desert, sending it a further 151 km (94 miles) to join, at Sharifkhansh, the line from Djulfal (on the Armenian frontier) to Tabriz and Teheran. One of the few settlements on this stretch of the journey is at Kotur, not very far from Lake Urmia, which is almost as large as Lake Van. This section was opened in 1971 when for some years an Iranian first-class couchette car and TCDD first-class car covered the 3,059 km (1,901 miles) from Istanbul to Teheran in three days and two nights. A diner was included on the section Razi to Teheran.

Iran had no railways until World War II, when British engineers built a line from Nader Sharpur on the Persian Gulf, via Teheran, to Bandar Shah on the Black Sea. This was to be a means of moving supplies to the Soviet Union, an

● LEFT
A former German war engine at the head of a typical Turkish "mixed" train, which conveys a combination of passenger-coaches and freight-wagons.

INFORMATION BOX

THE VAN GOLU EXPRESS	
Termini	Istanbul and Teheran
Countries	Turkey and Iran
Distance	3,059 km (1,901 miles)
Date of opening	1965

alternative to the perilous North Sea/ Baltic Sea convoys. The line to Djulfa, from where a Russian-gauge line ran to Erevan and beyond, was completed later.

With the overthrow of the Shah in 1979 and the Kurdish uprising in Iran and Turkey, the passenger service was discontinued. There are just a few local trains between Van and Kapikoy, but no Iranian ones. The line is risky, if not dangerous, and with growing road traffic, freight seems to have ceased too. The TCDD still operates the Van Golu from Istanbul to Tatvan three days a week.

● ABOVE
One of Turkey's most common steam designs, which was found at work all over the country, with a former German Kriegslokomotiv. These were the war engines of which some 6,000 were built to a basic design to aid Germany's war effort in World War II.

● ABOVE
The inauguration train of the Bandar Abbas BAFGH Railway in Iran.

● RIGHT
A typical double-headed Turkish steam train, with a German-built 4-8-0 piloting an express passenger 2-8-2 Mikado built by Henschel in 1937.

BASRA TO BAGHDAD

● LEFT
Baghdad railway station.

● BELOW LEFT
A Syrian Railways 2-8-0 built by Borsig of Berlin in 1914 during that builder's "British phase", in operation south of Damascus.

For all practical purposes, railways began in the land once called Mesopotamia during its Turkish Empire days, just as the Ottoman rule was coming to an end. However, it was the British Army, taking Mesopotamia early on in World War I, who laid most of the rail system, which operates to this day. Oil-rich Iraq embarked, together with Syria, on an expansion programme of its railways with faster trains linking Damascus with Baghdad on the historic line built by the Kaiser's Germany for the Ottoman Turks in the 1909–13 period. The line is of standard gauge and continues across the desert to Basra on the Gulf. Today rail services are sparse, with train speeds averaging scarcely 48 kph (30 mph) for "fast mails". The fastest trains run the 542 km (337 miles) between Basra and Baghdad in 11 hours.

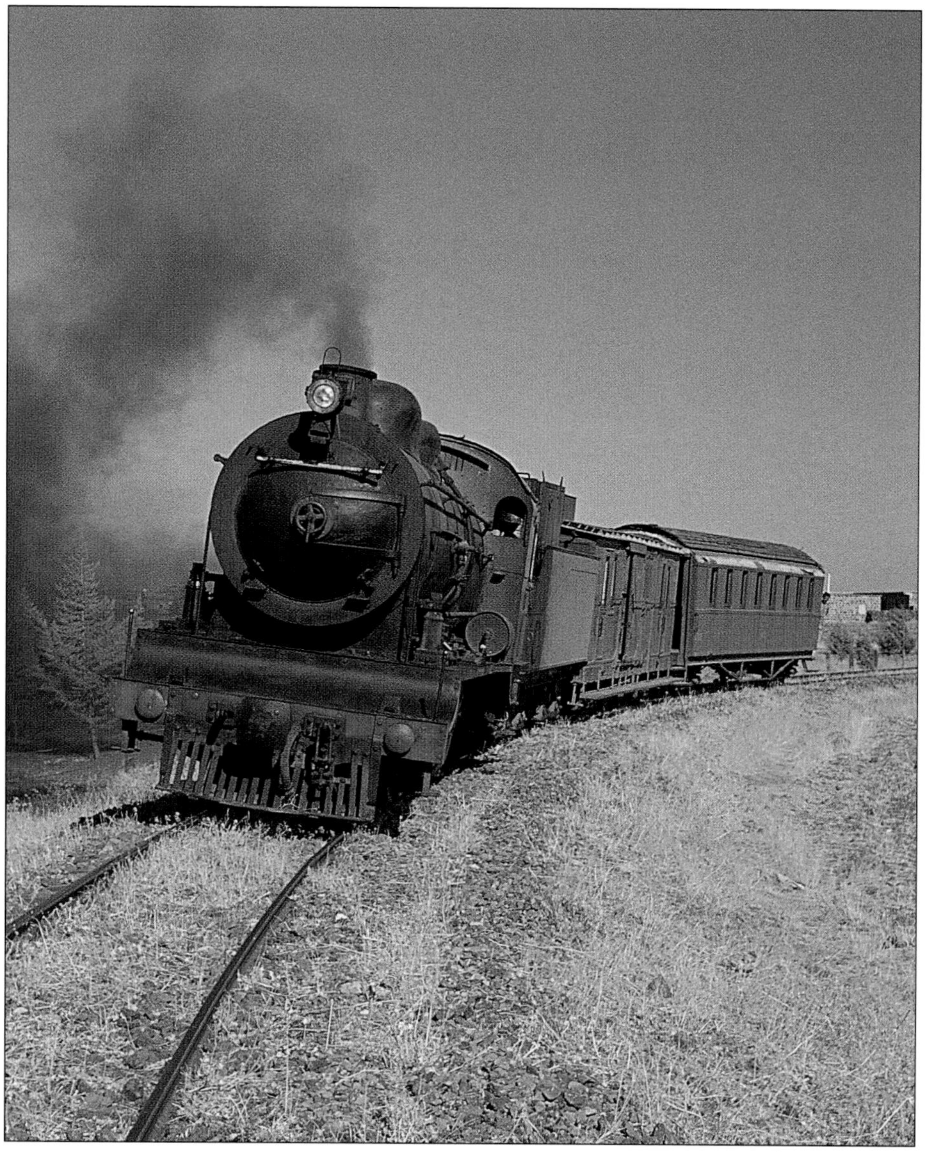

INFORMATION BOX

Termini	Basra and Baghdad
Country	Iraq
Length	542 km (337 miles)
Date of opening	1914

Passenger-trains on the Trans-Iranian line have their southern terminus at Khorramshah though the track goes through to Abadan, or Banda Khomeini, as it is now called. Technically an island, Abadan, seat of the great oil pipeline terminus and refinery, is a few miles further on. When it was demolished by the Turks at the beginning of the 19th century, on the grounds that Khorramshah's commercialism was detrimental to nearby Basra, the British and Russian governments stepped in to keep the peace by allocating territory to both sides. However, they reckoned without the Kuran River, a tributary of the Shatt-al-Arab, which promptly upped and changed its course, inserting a damp spanner into the works. As recent history has shown with a vengeance, nobody was

happy with the results. Basra, once in Iran, is now of course an Iraqi city, but the hate continues, and this was going great guns when I arrived in Khorramshah and wanted to reach Basra. I got there in the end by walking for miles across a no man's land of a desert, delayed lengthily and not very pleasantly by innumerable checkpoints and gun-toting soldiers.

A bevy of friendly Iraqis took charge of me in Basra, a city I found to be a hotchpotch of other people's developments: Carmathian, Mongol, Turk and European, with a thin veneer of Muslim. At the railway station I ran the station-master to ground, was invited to tea and finally – he learning of my inability to change my Barclays-issued traveller's cheque into local currency (Barclays being pronounced a "Lackey of Israel") – was given a first-class ticket valid for the air-conditioned deluxe overnight express to Baghdad.

From Basra to the Iraqi capital it is 611 km (380 miles), and the distance was covered in nine hours, which is a good rate of knots for a Middle Eastern train. For some way the route follows the Euphrates River and passes within two miles of Ur, of the Chaldees fame. We also flashed by a short platform designated "Babylon Halt" which apparently even the little local trains pass with a derisive whistle.

My berth was almost up to European standards, and after weeks of rough living and travelling on lesser trains and even lesser buses and lorries, it seemed like paradise. In the morning the train drew into West station, the Grand Central of the Iraqi capital.

ABOVE
A Syrian-built 2-6-0 tank dating back to the 1890s heads away from Damascus with a Sunday excursion train.

LEFT
After the day's intense sun the evening's mellow light brings relief to the border country between Syria and Lebanon as a Swiss-built 2-6-0 tank heads towards Damascus with an evening passenger-train.

Damascus to Medina

Every Muslim male is required to visit Muhammad's birthplace in Mecca at least once in his lifetime if he can. During the 19th century, the journey was hazardous in the extreme. The Arabs were reluctantly under Ottoman rule, and bands of vulnerable Turkish pilgrims were murdered as they journeyed through the desert. Eventually the Sultan of Turkey authorized the building of a railway between Damascus and Mecca to carry pilgrims in safety. Construction began in 1901, and seven laborious years later Medina, where Muhammad is buried, was reached 1,302 km (809 miles) to the south. This line, the Hedjaz, takes its name from the area alongside the Red Sea in Arabia where the holy city lies.

Trouble dogged every mile; marauding Arabs attacked the workers; the heat was intolerable, and violent sandstorms frequently caused work to be stopped. The Arabs, frantic that their holy city would be defiled, refused to allow the railway past Medina. In wild fervour they invaded the railway construction camp and massacred the work-force. The line was destined to go no further, and pilgrims had to continue on foot over the remaining 370 km (230 miles) to Mecca.

The railway only carried pilgrims for seven seasons until the outbreak of World War I. The Turks allied with Germany, and Arab nationalists, supported by the British under Colonel Lawrence, partly succeeded in driving the Turks from the Hedjaz. To prevent enemy reinforcements from getting through, Lawrence blew up large sections of the line. Indeed, so great was the damage that trains were forced to terminate at Ma'an in Southern Jordan. Today, almost 70 years later, not only does the southern section remain abandoned despite various attempts to reopen it, but many of the abandoned locomotives still lie half-buried in the sand.

The line now passes through three countries, and all would benefit by its reinstallation. In 1963 a consortium of

• ABOVE
A 2-8-2 crossing the desert, about 48 km (30 miles) from Amman. Although passenger traffic was ended by the Syrians in 1983, the line reopened for passenger traffic in 1987.

• LEFT
Nippon Pacific No. 82 storming up the bank out of Amman.

● RIGHT
A 2-8-2 pauses at Mafraq near the Syrian border. There is a twice-weekly service between the two countries, both for freight and passengers.

British engineers began work. The task was daunting. The section from Ma'an to Medina is 845 km (525 miles) long and, apart from being plagued by the elements (and damage incurred by Lawrence), 48 km (30 miles) of embankment had been washed away by the violent rains that sweep over the Arabian desert every five years. Half the route needed attention with much of the track unserviceable.

Much work had been done by 1967, when the Arab-Israeli War broke out and Saudi officials ordered work to stop. Work on the line was never resumed, and the railway was again abandoned with only the 467 km (290 mile) 3 ft $5^{1}/_{4}$ in gauge line section from Damascus to Ma'an remaining in operation.

INFORMATION BOX

Termini	Damascus and Medina
Country	Jordan to Saudi Arabia
Distance	1,302 km (809 miles)
Date of opening	1908

● LEFT
A 2-8-2 crosses a viaduct at a town near Amman.

● BELOW
Nippon Pacific No. 82 on the viaduct on the outskirts of Amman.

Moscow to Vladivostok
The Trans-Siberian Express

It was in 1858 that proposals were first made for a Trans-Siberian Railway that would connect Moscow and European Russia to the Pacific. Owing to the Crimean War, however, it was not until 1875 that an official plan was put forward. During the ensuing years other plans were proposed until, in 1891, the Russian Government finally gave its official approval, and Crown Prince Nicholas cut the first sod in Vladivostok. The railway, one of the world's greatest engineering achievements, was seen by the Russian Government as a means of consolidating the Russian hold on Siberia and the Pacific provinces by both developing the Eastern economy and exerting a political influence on China.

LEFT
Yaroslav station, Komsomol Square, Moscow. Built by the architect Franz Shekhiel in 1906, this is the western terminus of the Trans-Siberian Railway.

BELOW
The Kremlin and the River Moskva in Moscow.

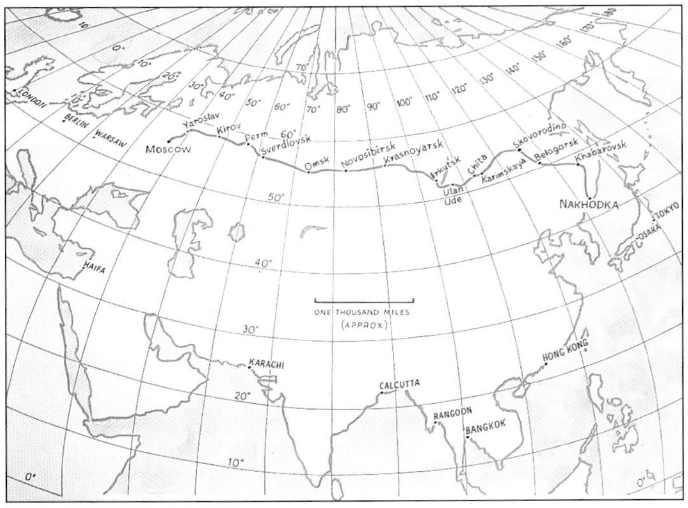

FAR LEFT
Map showing the route of the Trans-Siberian Railway.

LEFT
People queuing at a food and drink kiosk at Gorky Park, Moscow.

BELOW LEFT
The Rossia waits at Khabarovsk.

Although work began in 1891, through rail communication was only established in 1903. This did, however, include the train ferry over Lake Baikal – the deepest lake in the world. In the winter, when the ice became too thick for ice breaking, rails were laid on the ice itself and the train was run over the lake. The line round the southern shore of the lake was not blasted out of the solid rock until 1905. Such was the terrain of this 68 km (42 mile) section that no fewer than 38 tunnels had to be bored. In places, the shore of the lake is almost vertical and up to 1,200 m (4,000 ft) high. The toughest gradient is just east of Ulan Ude, where a sharp incline of 1:57.5 is encountered.

At first, part of the route was laid across Manchuria (and known as the Chinese Eastern Railway) direct from Chita via Harbin to Vladivostok. This section over Chinese soil was necessary because the comparatively flat land of Manchuria made the line both cheaper and shorter. However, after the Russo-Japanese War, which strained the line to capacity by carrying large numbers of troops and supplies from European Russia to the Far East, a connection was built from Chita via the Amar valley and Khabarovsk. Although considerably longer than the direct route across Manchuria, it did ensure that the whole route was over Russian territory.

Although the line, which begins at Moscow, goes through Omsk, Irkutsk (near the shores of Lake Baikal) and Khabarovsk before terminating at Vladivostok, was originally built as single track, by 1913 most of it had been

RIGHT
The Trans-Siberian Express, one of the world's greatest engineering achievements, and a railway legend.

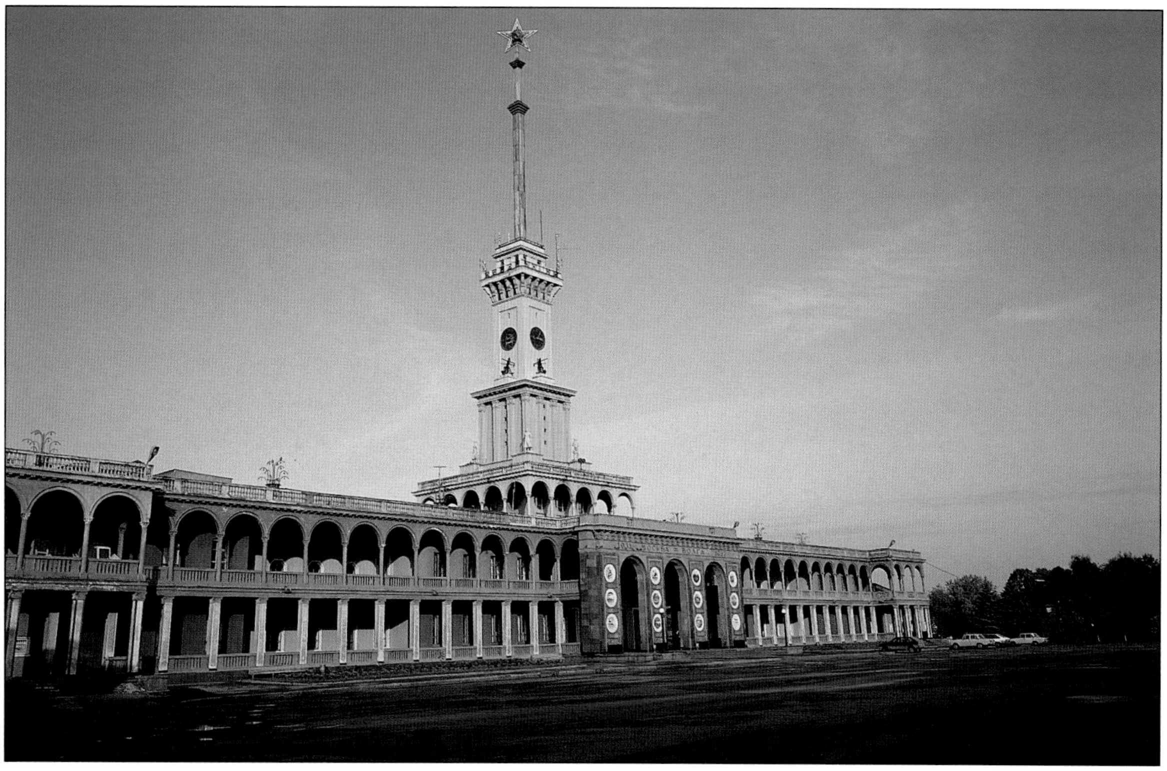

- LEFT
The archways and tower of the River Station, Moscow.

- BELOW LEFT
The railway bridge, built between 1896 and 1901, over the River Ob at Novosibirsk. It consists of seven main spans and is 814 m (2,670 ft) long.

- BELOW RIGHT
The Trans-Siberian Express at Chita.

converted to double track. It was not until the 1950s, however, that the whole route was double-tracked. By the mid-1970s, three-quarters of the line (from the European end) had been electrified.

One of the most interesting features of the line is the number of bridges. On the western portion of the line alone there are eight bridges of over 305 m (1,000 ft) in length, including those over the Irtish, the Ob and the Yenisei, all of which are over 610 m (2,000 ft), while at Khabarovsk, on the North Manchurian frontier, there is another exceptionally long bridge across the River Amur.

Between the two world wars, the through passenger service was provided by the Trans-Siberian Express, which had a special sleeping car and dining facilities. There was also the Blue Express, which included ordinary "hard" and "soft" accommodation as well as a sleeping car. These trains, which were relatively light, with only eight or nine carriages, took just under ten days to complete the 9,611 km (5,973 mile) journey from Moscow to Vladivostok, at an average speed of only 40 kph (25 mph).

In 1913, an English traveller called Pearson wrote a detailed account of the

journey, which began at Moscow's Yaroslav station. His train, headed by a highly polished Pacific locomotive, was composed of long green-and-gold carriages. The corridors were carpeted, and the dining car was decorated with an impressive ivory-white ceiling, large plate-glass windows and panelling. In those days the train also included a travelling bathroom, a chemist's shop and reading and games rooms.

Nine days on a train might not be everybody's ideal trip. Yet there are rail enthusiasts who say they dream of riding the Trans-Siberian Express. The author's experience of it when the country was still the Soviet Union, was not entirely the stuff of dreams. Although the four-bunk soft-class (Westerners were forbidden to travel hard-class) compartments were spacious and clean, there was a radio loudspeaker, which exuded the sort of thing expected from Stalinist Russia. The quality of everything, from coat-hangers to reading matter, was extremely poor. Moreover, the electric locomotive was Czech, and the silvery coaches were East German. Indeed, it would not be too far wrong to say that it was only the tea, served in the carriages from an old-fashioned samovar, that was genuinely Russian.

• ABOVE
Travellers at the railway station, Moscow.

• LEFT
The "Rossia" Trans-Siberian Express (left) in company with the Peking Express. Both trains had been halted by an accident on the line, just west of Irkutsk.

• BELOW LEFT
A traditional Russian wooden house.

INFORMATION BOX

THE TRANS-SIBERIAN EXPRESS

Termini	Moscow and Vladivostock
Country	Russia
Distance	9,611 km (5,972 miles)
Date of opening	1903

BRUSSELS TO HONG KONG

There is no such animal as a Trans-Siberian Express listed in the Russian Railway timetables or, for that matter, in any issue of the *Thomas Cook Overseas Timetable*. What you will see, however, is a Train No. Two, which travels between Moscow's Yaroslav station and Vladivostok's Main station. There are also other numbered trains with names like Baikal, Rossia and Tomich, which cover major sections of the 9,297 km (5,777 mile) line.

All these could be termed "Trans-Siberian Expresses", though to cover the route of the so-called Red Arrow Express – a collection of different trains running between Brussels and Hong Kong – the Baikal, linking Moscow to Irkutsk, was used on this section of the journey.

● LEFT
The Irkutsk to Moscow coach nameplate on the Baikal Express.

To attain Moscow from Brussels, the Ost West Express is the most convenient vehicle. This train leaves the Midi Station at 15.55 and arrives at Moscow Smolenskaya at 22.05 two nights later. It is now considerably faster and more comfortable than it used to be during the Communist era, when gruelling checks by border guards in the then German Democratic Republic, Poland and the then Soviet Union held up progress for hours – in addition to the still continuing

● BELOW
The train speeds through the Polish countryside.

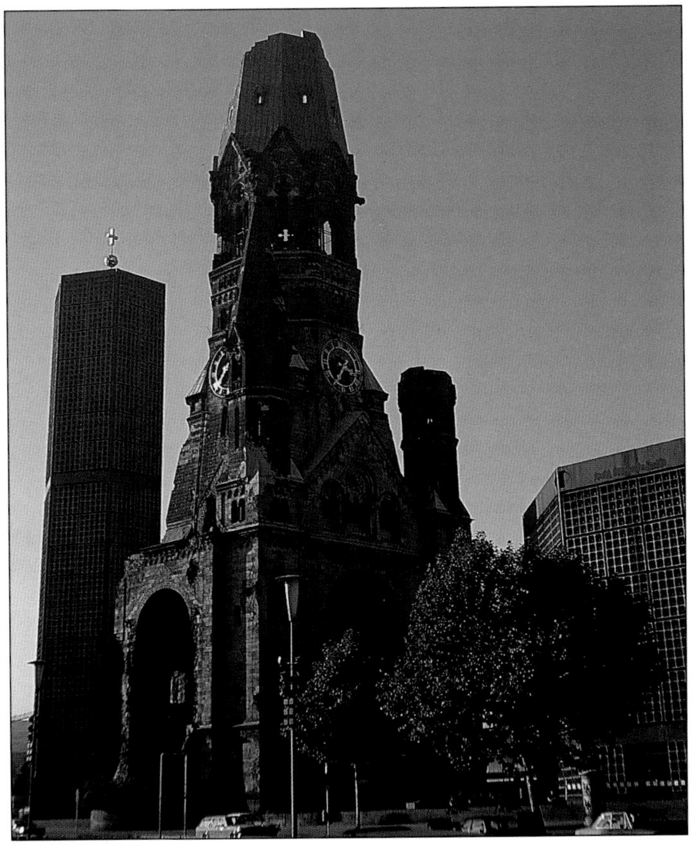

● RIGHT
Berlin's Frauen Kirche has been left as it was after being bombed in the Second World War as a reminder of the horrors of war.

INFORMATION BOX

Termini	Brussels and Kowloon
Countries	Belgium to Hong Kong
Distance	21,384 km (13,290 miles)
Date link completed	1949

chore of bogey-changing that is effected at Brest to adapt the train to the wider Russian gauge.

On the Trans-Siberian line, the long-distance expresses are reasonably comfortable, with soft- and hard-class berths that can be used as beds. Tea is always on tap from coach samovars and is brought to compartments by the attendants. The best time to traverse Siberia is autumn, when the seemingly endless landscape of birch trees turns to the colour of burnished gold. Crossing great rivers, such as the Ob and the Yenisei, on immense bridges makes for the most emotive sights.

Four days out, by which time the fare in the restaurant car has been reduced to mainly bortsch, macaroni and Russian champagne, the express reaches Irkutsk, capital of Siberia, and a not unattractive city with some timber houses of the Chekhov era still surviving. Here the

● LEFT
A Russian train approaches a country station.

● **RIGHT**
An interior coach view of the Ulan Bator to Peking express.

● **BOTTOM**
A view from the train window of the countryside of Outer Mongolia.

through coaches bound for Ulan Bator, the Mongolian capital, or – once weekly – right through to Beijing, are transferred to what was termed the Irkutsk-Ulan Bator Express. Maybe things have changed for the better, but the train used to be as dirty as the blankets issued for sleeping. From Ulan Ude, on the Russian-Mongolian border, the train was headed by a rust-pink – more rust than pink – diesel unit of Mongolian Railways to deflect southwards from the shores of Lake Baikal, snaking into the low hills and across rolling plains, the habitat of wild camels, wild horses and the Gobi bear. Occasional wind-swept villages of hexagonal *yurts* draw the eye. The line here is non-electric.

Ulan Bator's most attractive building is its small and well-kept station. The city itself is a dull one, centred on the standardized Soviet-style parade-ground square bordered by grim government buildings but enlivened in recent years by a pink stock-exchange. Though there is only one through train a week to Beijing, there are two a week from Ulan Bator to the Chinese capital.

The author's onward journey towards China was made in Chinese rolling stock. This was a step up in the comfort stakes, with shaded table lamps, jasmine-flavoured tea in flasks, dainty seat coverlets and chintzy curtains.

At Erlan, 36 hours later, the train bogeys have to be changed back to fit China's standard gauge, an operation that can be watched by passengers so inclined. Then, powered by a new and electric locomotive, the train enters the Chinese province of Inner Mongolia.

Railway construction in China has been considerable in recent years. By the time of the so-called liberation in 1949, only 11,000 km (6,835 miles) of rail track were still open to traffic, the remainder having been destroyed by many years of internal conflict. The total rail system now exceeds 55,000 km

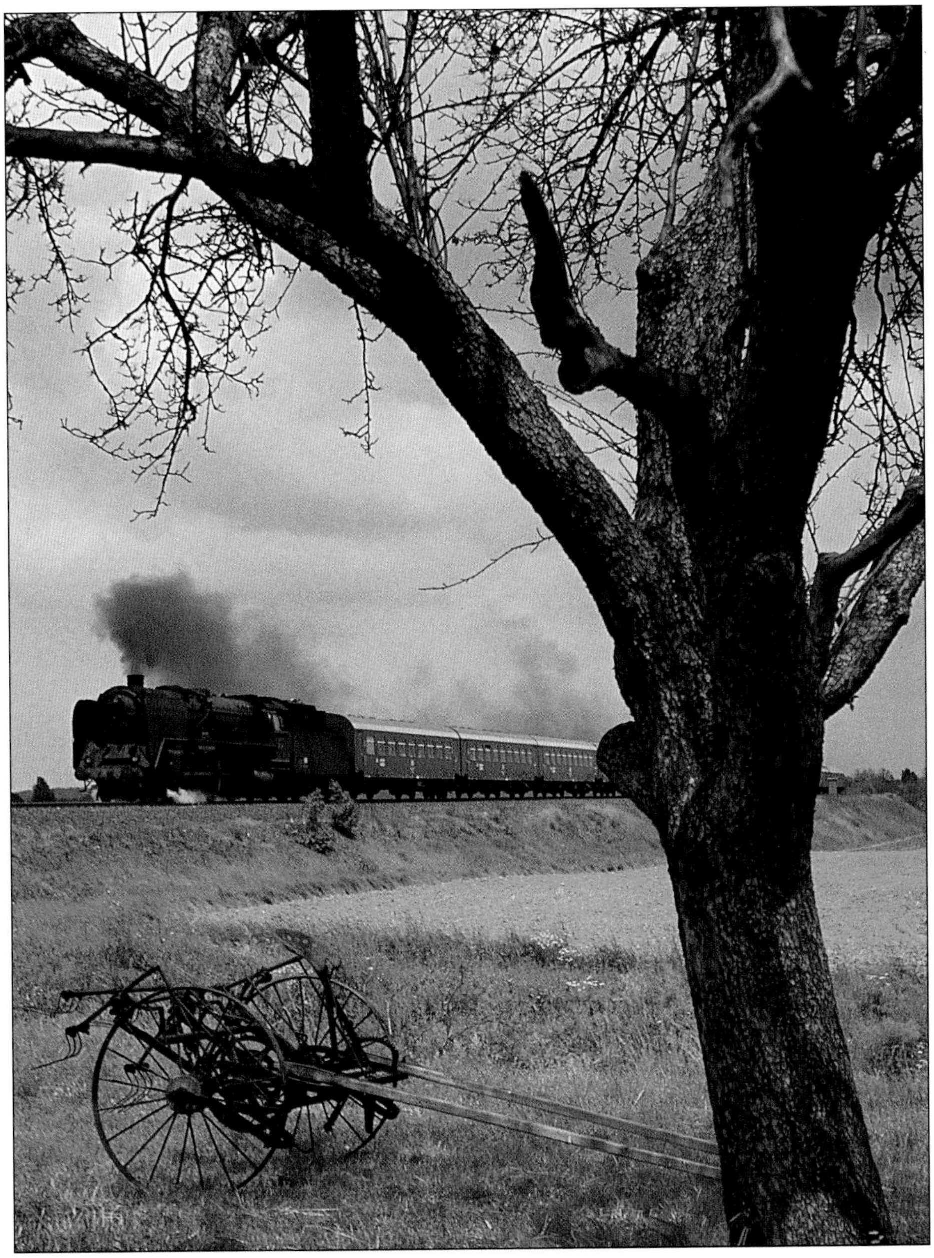

● LEFT
A train speeds through the old East Germany.

● BOTTOM
The Ulan Bator Express passing through the wooded hill country of Outer Mongolia.

(34,000 miles) and while, before 1949, seven provinces had no railways at all, now only Tibet is without rail communication – though the line to Lhasa has long been under construction.

Datong is a familiar name on account of its huge factory that produced those giant Chinese steam locomotives, but, alas, it is no longer doing so. Visitors were once lucky enough to be shown around the works when these monsters were in full production and, if they were very lucky, even allowed to drive a newly produced locomotive undergoing its operational testing. China's capital, Beijing, is not the largest city in the country – that accolade goes to Shanghai – but the trappings of capitalship lie firmly upon the city's shoulders. The main station is a surprisingly modest establishment, constantly overcrowded. From Beijing southwards the train is electric powered, and for another 36 hours one can enjoy eminently comfortable living quarters and often delicious scenery to match. The 2,400 km (1,500 mile) route lies through sprawling cities and over prodigious rivers, such as the Yangtse, where trains clatter endlessly across great bridges.

Before Canton, round-topped peaks give the lie to the idea that Chinese landscape paintings are figments of Chinese imagination, and provide an intensely beautiful finale to the journey. Here the line cuts through the gorges of the Pei Kiang and a water-logged territory of rice paddies peopled by half-submerged peasants and water buffalo.

The ride from Canton to Hong Kong is the smoothest of all. And there is nothing like a three-week rail journey to give the luxurious comforts of this unique Anglo-Chinese city an added lustre.

Quetta to Zaheidan Across the Baluchistan Desert

- BELOW LEFT
The village of Skardu.

- BOTTOM
One of Pakistan's diesel-electrics, which haul international services.

The lonely line that connects Quetta to the southern Iranian town of Zaheidan is known by some as the Nushki Extension Railway though it runs hundreds of kilometres past Nushki, across the border and 80 km (50 miles) into Iran. It leaves Quetta's main line at Spezand and continues parallel to the mountain ranges forming the frontier with Afghanistan. The line was laid during World War I, when the British and Russians "policed" the territory between the Caspian Sea and the Persian Gulf.

Between Dalbandin and Nok Kundi, a distance of 167 km (104 miles), the region is wholly without habitation, virtually devoid of vegetation and a hell upon earth. The line crosses long stretches of desert covered with sharp black stones broken only by patches of

coarse sand. For eight months of the year the heat is intense, and the "120-day wind" whips this sand into tight little whirlwinds that lacerate the skin. The whole desert is covered with sulphur dust, and water, when it is obtainable, tastes like a concentrated mixture of common and Epsom salts. When there is any rain at all, the whole year's fall may occur within an hour. The river beds, bone dry for 90 days out of 100, then hurl the water, laced with quantities of stone, at the exposed railway. To overcome this disconcerting event, the engineers built Irish bridges, or "dips", and the drivers of the steam-hauled trains crossing them were expected to use their discretion as to whether they could pass through without water getting into their fireboxes and putting the fire out.

Then there are the *do-reg*, or marching sand-hills. These are crescent-shaped sand-hills formed by the wind and constantly on the move. Again the line is the target and, from time to time, diversionary track has to be laid to take

● LEFT
The river Indus.

● BELOW
A typical Pakistani tea shop at Skardu.

the railway round the back of the *do-reg* to avoid several thousand tonnes of sand. The sand-hills move in parallel lines for many miles across the *dasht*. Their speed is 500–600 m (1,600–1,900 ft) per year, so the duplicated tracks are left in position and trains use whichever one happens to be clear of sand.

Sometimes the marching sand-hills cover the track, and then all the male passengers from the stranded train spend hours re-laying the track. Spare lengths of rail, shoes and sleepers lie alongside in readiness for just an emergency. These, then, are just some of the vicissitudes of a trans-Baluchistan journey.

Hours behind schedule, the journey will be resumed across the terrible landscape. At a remote habitation, the train halts for what seems to the weary passengers an interminable period while the crew is changed.

At Mirjaveh, on the Iranian border, there is a long passport check and general evacuation to the hut for the issue of Iranian railway tickets for the last 80 km (50 miles) to Zaheidan, which is reached – if there are no delays such as those mentioned above – some 30 hours after departure from Quetta.

INFORMATIONBOX

Termini	Quetta and Zaheidan
Countries	Pakistan and Iran
Distance	650 km (404 miles)
Date of opening	1916

● LEFT
Young boys working in the fields at Tongul.

Lindi Kotal to Peshawar Down the Khyber

It is probably only the British who become charged with emotion at the mere mention of the Khyber Pass. Its fame is based on history rather than scenery, and the comparatively recent and universally known story of the Khyber is exclusively British – though the armies of Alexander the Great and the Mogul emperors Babur and Humayan also used its defiles.

The British-built line climbs to about 1,070 m (3,500 ft) on wide-gauge track without rack-and-pinion assistance, and even with two engines it is heavy going. From Lindi Kotal there was a once-weekly train to Peshawar run at no charge, simply as a gesture by Pakistan Railways to prove to the fiercely independent tribesmen that the line, in spite of them, was open and the Pakistan Government was the boss.

The old coaches were a morass of humanity intent upon going along for the free ride. With not an inch of space available, the author found a seat astride the right-hand front buffer of a steam locomotive made by the British Vulcan foundry in 1923. Two Pakistani passengers had already seated themselves on the other buffer, and a necklace of humanity encircled the boiler.

The 64 km (40 mile) ride that followed was a spectacular and unforgettable journey. The descent of the Khyber is the steepest non-rack stretch of track in the world. It is made in the form of a letter Z, the train changing

● **LEFT**
Passengers stretch their legs in the heat of the afternoon.

INFORMATION BOX

Termini	Lindi Kotal and Peshawar
Country	Pakistan
Distance	64 km (40 miles)
Date of opening	1902

● **BELOW LEFT**
Locomotive No. 2495 steams through a cutting in the red hills of western Pakistan.

● **BELOW RIGHT**
Tribal musicians meet travellers at the Khyber Pass.

● LEFT
The train takes a curve in this typical western Pakistan landscape.

● BELOW LEFT
The Pakistan/ Afghan border at the Khyber Pass.

● BELOW RIGHT
An armed guard stands by the regimental coats of arms in the Khyber Pass.

direction at each apex and, on the steepest sections, safety track is installed to divert runaway trains into the hills. Until one became accustomed to the motion, one felt extremely insecure astride the metal seat. To maintain balance, it was necessary to grip the greasy ironwork with one's knees with hands clamped to the buffer flanges like limpet mines. The great hissing, threatening boiler licked the passengers with jets of steam, while one's imagination worked overtime painting mind pictures of what the relentless wheels would do to anyone who had the misfortune to fall off.

The train travelled at no great pace through a series of short tunnels and beneath empty forts, which gave a walnut topping to every brown hill. The Khyber's narrowest defile was commanded by the oldest of these – Ali Masjid – built high on a cliff, and near to it was a showcase displaying regimental badges, British, Pathan and Indian.

All around was an alien landscape, burnt brown and exuding that air of latent hostility so different from the green meadows of England. Here was magnificence for sure, but its constituents were sharply formed crags varying in shades of colour from deep red to sandy yellow, punctuated by jagged pinnacles of rock.

The plain below the pass was suddenly upon the train, the brown and barren hills abruptly deflated. Fortified villages, their high mud walls blank apart from firing slits, remained in evidence, their unseen occupants presumably still ready to repulse attack from wherever it might come. At one point, where the line doubled back on itself, one could see the Khyber mountain looking impregnable to man and train; not a gap or defile showed anywhere. The train limped into Peshawar, the once-in-a-lifetime vice-regal ride at an end.

Kalyan to Howrah Across India by Troop Train

One of the great experiences in life is to travel across a mighty land mass such as the Indian subcontinent, as it was known in 1945. This account is based on notes made at the time, but the expanded version was lost to the military censor because of the railway details it contained. Some things have changed dramatically since then, but the long history and traditions of the many peoples of that great land mass will ensure that much also remains the same.

It was not a journey made voluntarily, but as a soldier under orders, heading for the advance HQ of the Allied Land Forces in South-east Asia – wherever that might be. In the meantime, the railway and its surroundings were there to be enjoyed or endured as the case may be.

The author had landed at Bombay some weeks before and had travelled several times between there and Kalyan, using trains that were generally hauled by massive 2-C0-1 electric locomotives, built in 1925 by Metropolitan Vickers of the UK for the Great Indian Peninsular Railway standard (5 ft 6 in) gauge and operating on a line voltage of 1,500 d.c.

● LEFT
One of the large electric locomotives of the Great Indian Peninsular Railway easing a train from Kalyan into Victoria terminus, Bombay, in March 1945.

INFORMATION BOX

Termini	Kalyan and Howrah
Country	India
Distance	2,129 km (1,323 miles)
Date of travel	1945

● BELOW LEFT
A train load of cotton in a timeless scene.

● BELOW RIGHT
A train crosses a bridge while a young woman sits by the river with her water pot.

It was probably one such that was hauling the troop train, consisting of 14 coaches and two vans, a load of some 567 tonnes (560 tons) tare, which left Kalyan at 1100 hours on 8 March 1945.

The line was fairly level and straight as it passed through rather arid country, which allowed for speeds up to 113 kph (70 mph). Although I was travelling in third class, it was not overcrowded and the compartment was large. Windows that came right down and shutters to keep out the glare of the sun, coupled with the speed of the train, made things

● BELOW
A train crosses a river using one of the many bridges on the Indian rail network.

● BELOW
A contemporary photograph of a scene that is virtually unchanged since 1946.

● BOTTOM
A train steams through the Indian countryside.

reasonably comfortable, although the well-shaped wooden seats encouraged movement from time to time. There was no through corridor connection, which meant that lengthy stops were required so that one could collect the meals provided and wash personal utensils and mess tins in the vats provided.

At the approach to the Western Ghats, just beyond Khardi, hard climbing began, with the line twisting and turning and passing through several tunnels. It got colder, and wonderful views opened up of the plain below, followed by spectacular engineering as the line clung to steep valley sides.

At Igatpuri, electricity gave way to steam haulage, and it is possible that traction was put in the hands of a Class XA1 4-6-2 built by Vulcan Foundry in the UK in 1929. From here the line undulated over a rather barren plain dotted with villages until arrival at Deolalih, a feared posting for army troops, which gave its name to doolally, a nickname for a form of madness.

Soon after departure from Deolalih, the train began the long drag of some 80 km (50 miles) at gradients of 1:200 to 1:120 to the 914 m (2,999 ft) summit of the line. At that time of the year, in the dry season, the scene was forbiddingly barren but enlivened by hawks circling above looking for prey.

During the night, the train stopped at Sonepur, at a station that proclaimed that it had the longest platform in India, and then at the major city of Nagpur, where locomotives were changed, the system from here on being the Bengal Nagpur Railway.

By morning, the train was descending, twisting and turning past sheer rock faces. Toward the end of the day, the countryside became more green until jungle pressed upon the line. By night, it can be very cold, but the temperature soon rises with the sun and the hot, steamy conditions were such as to encourage us to sit with our feet over the footsteps of the carriage, which provided some interesting experiences when the train crossed high bridges over rivers or dried water-courses with an unobstructed view of the ground below.

As night fell, flat country was again encountered. In the night, the sight of the enormous Tatanagar steel works left a lasting impression. By morning, the train was on double track some 80 km (50 miles) from Calcutta in low-lying, dank and misty marshland, cold in the early light. Lines proliferated, and we passed local trains crammed with people with others on the outsides and on the roofs of carriages.

Howrah station, 2,129 km (1,323 miles) and 44 hours from Kalyan, was a sea of people, with porters vying to carry passengers' luggage to waiting rickshaws and taxis. As the crossing of India came to a close, one was left with wonderful memories of a truly unique rail journey set in unbelievable scenery.

DELHI TO COCHIN

Amid the chaos that characterizes all Indian railway stations, New Delhi's contains an air-conditioned haven that is the Foreigners' Booking Office, where comparative order is preserved. From here you can set out, armed perhaps with that open-sesame of Indian rail travel, the Ind-Rail Pass, on a journey south on the second longest rail route in the country.

The vehicle for much of the way is the Kerala Express. The train is not one of the "super expresses" that ply between Delhi and Bombay, but, while never generating great speed, its progress is reasonable enough. At intervals small flasks of tea and hot meals – ordered prior to delivery (vegetarian or "European") at ridiculously low cost – are served, and, come nightfall, the compartment seats are turned into bunks.

The route is not initially a spectacular one, the urban centres being Agra, Gwalior, Jhansi, Bhopol, Nagpur, Gudin, Coimatore and Cochin. The last of these is in the province of Kerala, its distinctive woods, lakes and coconut plantations making a sudden and picturesque change from the parched flatlands of central India. At Trivandrum, the Keralan capital, a bed may be acquired for the night in a dormitory of that British-inspired and now firmly Indian concept called a railway retiring room. The cost again is infinitesimal and, should one be averse to the continual noises of snoring and hawking, private rooms are also available. Pillows, sheets and pillowcases are issued, and a lockable bedside cupboard is provided. A very welcome hot shower is also supplied.

From Cochin, a beautiful city of Portuguese ancestry overflowing on to a trio of islands, you can, if you choose, forgo the famed beaches of nearby

● **ABOVE**
The station in New Delhi, India's capital city since 1931.

● **LEFT**
Panan bridge under construction.

● **BELOW LEFT**
A group of railway workers zip along the tracks near Cochin station, southern India

INFORMATION BOX

Termini	Delhi and Cochin
Country	India
Distance	2,100 km (1,305 miles)
Commencement of building	1853

● **RIGHT AND BELOW**
The bustling station at Rameswaram station, the ferry port for Sri Lanka.

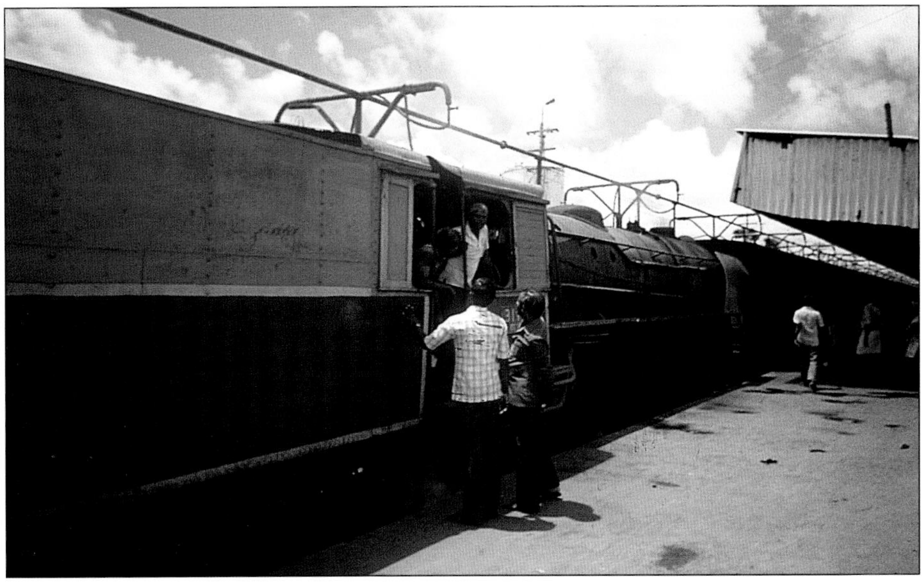

Kovalam, take the short train ride to Cape Comerin, the extreme southern tip of India, where three oceans meet.

Another ride can be taken southward to Rameswaram on the Madras-Rameswaram Express, which can be joined at Coimbatore. Rameswaram, with its sacred shrine, is a ferry port for Sri Lanka, just across the Palk Strait. The town is approached by the gigantic, recently built Panan bridge, over which the train slowly trundles. The same train, a day later, will take the traveller back as far as Madurai, to view its massive temple, prior to joining a night train to the garden city of Bangalore.

From Bangalore, one travels on to Mysore and northwards to, eventually, Coa and Bombay on a variety of trains with varying characteristics and degrees of comfort. Prior to Bombay it is worth pausing at Pune – Poona of British Army fame – which is the site of another narrow-gauge mountain line, the Matheran Hill Railway.

The return to Delhi is on the crack Rajdhani Express, which, by the standards of the Indian railway system, is of sublime comfort and high speed. On it, attendants make the beds, and afternoon tea, dinner, early morning tea and breakfast are all included in the price of the ticket. However, after travelling for weeks on lesser trains, you might find this rather a dull one, lacking the charm of the true India.

Delhi to Jodhpur
The Palace on Wheels

● **BELOW AND BENEATH**
The Fort of Jodhpur, one of the locomotives that hauls the Palace on Wheels.

Though the Raj is no more, the romance of the train lives on in India – or at least it does for many foreign visitors, Britons predominating. To cater for these nostalgic longings, Indian Railways in conjunction with the Rajasthan Tourist Board produced a train to resurrect a glamorous past. They called it the Palace on Wheels. Alas, this palace of a train is no more, but another in the same vein has taken its place. The "Palace" was assembled from appropriate coaches unearthed from sources throughout the subcontinent, many rusting away in obscure sidings and some once owned by long-deposed maharajas. Restored to their former glory, they became the pride and joy of Indian Railways.

What set the final seal of authenticity were the two superb steam locomotives chosen to head them. To complement the image of the golden coaches, these giant monsters with their shining brass-work, glistening pistons and proud coat of arms at the front of the boiler were christened Desert Queen and Fort of Jodhpur. Crews were hand-picked from the cream of drivers for this, the most prestigious train in all India.

On the inaugural journey, the coach, bearing the insignia of the Jaipur State Railway, was one which had once carried the Maharaja of Bikaner, while a more recent incumbent had been Mrs Gandhi, the late Indian Prime Minister. It was the most opulent and historic saloon of all, with pink upholstery, silver-embroidered curtains, teak wall panels and traditional carpeting. The suites consisted of a bedroom, amply proportioned, with a wide bed, a wardrobe and a bedside table, and a comfortable lounge, generously equipped with sofas and

INFORMATION BOX

The Palace on Wheels	
Termini	Delhi and Jodhpur
Country	India
Distance	250 km (155 miles)
Date of first run	1982

● **RIGHT**
The Palace on Wheels arriving at Jaisalmer.

● **BELOW**
A driver's-eye view of the track ahead of the Palace on Wheels.

armchairs. Two servants attired in turbans and smart Rajastani costumes were constantly at the guests' beck and call. Included in the train's make-up were a restaurant car serving gourmet dinners and fine wines, a lounge, observation car and library.

Rajasthan is a state made for such a train. Much of it is desert or semi-desert, but the towns of Jaipur, Udaipur, Jaisalmer, Jodhpur and Bharatpur are fairyland cities: pink-stoned, rock-pinnacled lakeside oases, dominated by fortresses and palaces, each flaunting an epic history engraved upon dramatically beautiful buildings.

Having rumbled through the night, the Palace would arrive at its destination where, after breakfast in bed, guests were invited to emerge on to the platform strewn with flowers, to be welcomed by a pipe band, elephants in regalia and troupes of dancing girls. Suitably garlanded, they would be whisked away for the tour of the day, broken by a superb lunch in a palace.

A none-too smooth metre-gauge track, emphatically not continuously welded, made sleep a little elusive for those not lulled by train travel, but this is to quibble. From the one-time centre of the Raj – Delhi – a traveller could begin a journey such as he or she was unlikely ever to experience again.

● **OPPOSITE BOTTOM**
The Palace on Wheels waiting at Rajasthan station.

● **RIGHT**
The Desert Queen, one of the locomotives that hauls the Palace on Wheels.

Siliguri to Darjeeling

The railway that takes passengers from the heat of the Bengal plains to the blissful mountain balm of Darjeeling involves a climb of no less than 2,164 m (7,100 ft) in a distance of 88 km (54½ miles). Before the railway was built in 1879, exiles from the heat had to take the cart-road, which had been built by the Government at an astronomical cost.

The track is 2 ft gauge and, remarkably, while train loads have to be restricted, is worked wholly by adhesion. The steel rails, which weigh 41 lb per yard, are laid on wooden sleepers. Because the track has to be lifted so much in such a short distance, heavy gradients and sharp curves are unavoidable. On the journey there are banks ranging from 1:19 to 1:31 and curves of 15 m (50 ft) radius.

For the first 11 km (7 miles) to Sookna the going is easy, as the ascent is only 1:281. It is on this stretch that the 213 m (699 ft) long Mahanuddy bridge, comprising seven 30 m (100 ft) spans, is crossed. It is when the train leaves Sookna that the climb begins in earnest, for in the next 7.6 km (4¾ miles) the track ascends 265 m (869 ft). At the end of this section, the ascent was so sudden that originally the track had to describe a sharp loop through a deep cutting. However, in 1883 part of the

INFORMATION BOX

Termini	Siliguri and Darjeeling
Country	India
Length	88 km (55 miles)
Date construction commenced	1879

ABOVE The train stops for a break and passengers take the opportunity to stretch their legs.

LEFT The little engine is inspected as it sits at the station.

OPPOSITE MIDDLE LEFT AND OPPOSITE MIDDLE RIGHT Various angles of the engine, which seems almost toy-like, that carries passengers from Siliguri to Darjeeling.

OPPOSITE BOTTOM At an altitude of 2,258 m (7,408 ft), Ghoom is the second highest main line station in the world.

● **RIGHT**
The sign welcoming visitors to the town of Darjeeling.

mountainside slipped into the cutting, completely filling it, and the track had to be realigned.

Between Rungtong, at 428 m (1,404 ft), and Tindharia, at 860 m (2,822 ft), a distance of just over 12 km (7½ miles), the gradient stiffens to 1:29. Just past Rungtong there is a sudden rise of 42 m (138 ft), which is overcome by what is practically a double loop that involves sharp curvatures. Then, a little further on, just before Tindharia, the ingenuity of the builders is illustrated by a "reverse". The line, climbing at a 1:28 gradient, enters a curve of 244 m (800 ft) radius, where it reaches a dead end at 754 m (2,474 ft). The train backs up a second curve at 1:33, to another dead end at 762 m (2,500 ft). After a further climb at 1:28, the line reaches an altitude of 773 m (2,536 ft).

The next section of the line, the 6.4 km (4 miles) between Tindharia and Gybaree, encounters the heaviest average gradient of the journey – 1:28. It is on this section that "Agony Point" is reached. Not only is the ascent steep but, because of the tight squeeze for space on the upper part of the loop, the train virtually overhangs the hillside as it negotiates a precipitous curve of 18 m (59 ft) radius.

After this challenging stretch, the route becomes less arduous, and once Gybaree is reached the gradients become slightly easier, a mere 1:32, for the 6.4 km (4 miles) to Mahanuddy, at 1,256 m (4,120 ft) above sea level. After Sonada, 66 km (41 miles) into the journey, comes one of the least exacting stretches of all – the 1:36 climb to the summit at Ghoom, 2,258 m (7,408 ft) above sea level. From here, the line descends to the city of Darjeeling and journey's end.

Kalka to Simla

- OPPOSITE TOP
The view, from the station, of Simla and beyond.
- BELOW
The lovingly maintained rail station at Simla.

The Simla Mail does not go to Simla at all. To reach this one-time British hill station, one has to leave the main line at Kalka and transfer to the white-painted railcar for the five-hour haul up through the green hills. As the passengers take their seats in this undramatic little train, carriage attendants solicitously wrap rugs around their legs, as it is still only five o'clock in the morning.

For much of the way the line runs close to the road, their paths crossing at frequent intervals. To enable trains to climb the 1,524 m (5,000 ft) to Simla, 3 km (2 miles) of viaducts and 107 tunnels had to be constructed over a track length of 96 km (60 miles), such is the terrain. Two hours out, and the train halts at the little station of Barog, where the railcar waits while its passengers partake of a leisurely breakfast before setting off again into the tumbling clouds.

INFORMATION BOX

Termini	Simla and Kalka
Country	India
Length	96 km (60 miles)
Date of opening	1903

Occasionally the cloud and mist are rent by shafts of light to reveal a valley floor hundreds of metres below, ignored by the busy little train, which has more important things than views on its mind as it hoots indignantly at buffalo and goats straying on to the track.

The Solan brewery halt is both a brewery and a station. The brewery came first, erected in the 19th century by a British company, which found good spring water here in the hills of Himachel Pradesh. In 1904, when the railway was built, the line cut right through the brewery, and passengers thereafter were treated to the rich aroma of malt and hops at the station approaches.

With each engaging of the gears, the little railcar gives a slight leap forward, reminiscent of the effects of "Kangaroo Petrol" when one is learning to drive a

car. In fact, the sight of this vehicle puts one in mind of a light blue Ford truck that has escaped from a museum. There are actually four such vehicles in service, built in 1927 and reconditioned in 1982.

The longest tunnel on the line is No. 33 at Barog, at a height of 1,144 m (3,753 ft) above sea level (at Kalka,) through which the train proceeds at the maximum permitted speed of 29 kph (18 mph). Including the viaducts, there are 869 bridges which gives an indication of the engineering problems faced during the construction of the line.

The car will halt at any station *en route* by request and – since there is no WC aboard – anywhere along the line for those passengers in urgent need. However, above Solan station there is something called a "Relieving Lodge", which presumably caters for more onerous bodily functions. Simla station, presents such a magnificent view down the mountains that the traveller feels amply rewarded for the $4\frac{1}{2}$ hour ride.

● **BELOW**
The Kalka to Simla railcar standing at Kalka station.

PULGAON TO ARVI

The Pulgaon to Arvi line, originally a narrow-gauge branch from the Great Indian Peninsular Railway, will go down in history as the last genuine narrow-gauge line in India. It leaves the Bombay to Nagpur 5 ft 6 in broad-gauge main line at Pulgaon, where it has its own little station next to the main-line one, to meander through remote cotton-growing country to the town of Arvi some 33 km (20 miles) away. Immediately alongside Pulgaon station is a massive 19th-century British cotton factory, a truly "dark satanic mill", which is blessed with a fabulous steam hooter poignantly reminiscent of the industrial north of Victorian England. It is likely that the origin of the line lay in conveying cotton from the outlying areas to this mill. India's only other surviving narrow-gauge, 2 ft 6 in main lines are the tourist-operated Darjeeling Himalayan Railway and the famous tourist line in the south

INFORMATION BOX

Termini	Pulgaon and Arvi
Country	India
Distance	33 km (20 miles)
Date of opening	1917

TOP The morning train, No. 643, leaves Pulgaon and passes a bullock-drawn cart of cotton bales heading for the factory next to the station.

ABOVE LEFT The ZP Pacific's driver in reflective mood at Arvi prior to working the evening train back to Pulgaon.

LEFT The afternoon train heads across the river at Kubgaon on the final leg of its journey to Arvi.

RIGHT
If running to time, the last train of the day reaches Rhona Town at sunset.

BELOW RIGHT
The timelessness of waiting for trains in India is epitomized by this rural scene at Sorta – the travellers all being resigned to a long dreary wait. Should a bus come along in the mean-time, many will take it rather than wait for the train.

based on Ootacamun (known as the "Ooty"). At one time the line had three daily mixed trains each way, along with an old Armstrong Whitworth diesel railcar of 1934. Today, with two daily trains each way, the line is distinctive in being worked by ZP Class Pacifics of traditional British design but built by Nippon in Japan in 1954. These sprightly locomotives, originally built for the Satpura lines but transferred in 1976, are some of the last Pacific locomotives in the world, certainly the last in India with the exception of the metre-gauge YP Class.

The appalling difficulties facing maintenance engineers with the shortage of spare parts means that only one locomotive is in steam at any one time, and the line has no crossing loops, although formerly a loop did exist at Rhona Town.

The line is a last vestige of a form of transport that was once common in many parts of the world and retains all the characteristics of a classic country railway of the late 19th century. Four trains a day are scheduled to run: No. 643 leaves Pulgaon at 08.00 and arrives in Arvi at 10.20; No. 644 leaves Arvi at 10.40 and reaches Pulgaon at 12.25; No. 645 leaves Pulgaon at 14.30 and reaches Arvi at 16.50; and No. 646 leaves Arvi at 17.30 and arrives in Pulgaon at 19.15.

There are nine stations on the route: Pulgaon, Sorta, Virol, Rhona Town, Dhanori, Pargothan, Pachegaon, Kubgaon

ABOVE
Poor coal is a perennial problem. These huge lumps of clinker have been shovelled out of the firebox following the fire grate becoming clogged and the engine failing to steam.

● **RIGHT**
Railway supremacy is asserted at this level crossing near Rhona as ZP Class Pacific No. 2 hustles its two coach train over the main road.

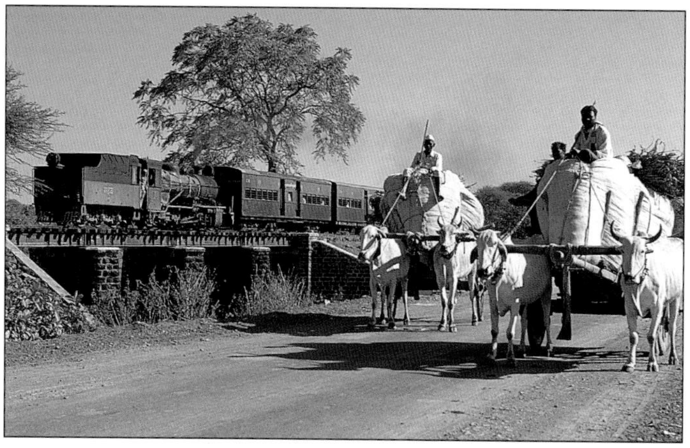

● **BELOW RIGHT**
The afternoon train from Pulgaon to Arvi overtakes a pair of carts bringing cotton in from the surrounding fields.

and Arvi. The line passes through remote countryside, and many of the stations are simple tin shacks in the middle of nowhere, the villages they serve being some some distance away. Rhona Town serves a sizeable community which has a large cotton mill, as does Kubgaon.

The line is paralleled throughout by a road, which is generally well surfaced and over which frequent buses ply their trade. They provide serious competition for the railway and prevent it from being profitable. The only supremacy the railway can claim lies in the many level crossings. This classic roadside tramway is picturesque and rustic, travellers being solely village people and mostly heavily laden ones who use the train to carry their bags of produce.

The trains consist of two bogie coaches and on the outward journey from Pulgaon the engines go tender first; upon reaching Arvi the coaches are shunted round to ensure that the brake remains at the rear of the consist.

It is said that one tonne of coal is burnt on the engine on each trip, which seems excessive for such a small locomotive so lightly laden. It is possible that, as with so many rural Indian lines that were worked by steam, coal is thrown down at strategic points along the track to favoured recipients in return for rupees!

The quality of the coal is another reason for sloth on the line, as much of it turns to clinker and clogs up the firebox, necessitating regular stops for "blow-ups". If coal is unavailable, all trains are cancelled. Likewise punctuality is treated very liberally – lateness can be caused either by mechanical problems or,

● **BOTTOM LEFT**
Monkeys play around the station name board at Arvi.

● **BOTTOM RIGHT**
The water pump outside the station at Pargothan attracts women from the surrounding villages. Here they are busily filling their urns as the morning train to Pulgaon prepares to depart for Arvi.

● LEFT
These buses plying the surfaced main road symbolize the threat posed by road competition.

● ABOVE
Travelling musicians entertaining passengers during the station stop at Sorta.

seemingly, the whims of the engine crew who have a frequent tendency of stopping for tea at Pargothan.

In today's world, the sheer joy of a railway such as this is always going to be under threat, and early in 1997 diesel servicing facilities were installed and ZDM4A No. 198 arrived from Kurduwadi. There was no immediate question of the diesel taking over, as many spare parts had to be obtained, and ZP Pacific No. 2 continued as before. Fortunately, despite the line's incredible unprofitability, Indian Railways have extended the contract with the British owners to operate the line up to 2006.

● BELOW
The picturesque rural nature and general remoteness of this country line can be gauged from this scene of the scrub and bush, which characterize much of the land.

Colombo to Kandy

This picturesque, and often thrilling railway line was built between 1858 and 1868 to link Colombo, the present capital, with the former capital of what was then Ceylon, Kandy, in the mountains 488 m (1,601 ft) above sea level and 121 km (75 miles) distant. The system expanded to 1,530 km (951 miles) at the standard gauge of 5 ft 6 in and 138 km (86 miles) at the narrow gauge of 2 ft 6 in, the latter mainly up the valley of the Kelani River. Mileage has now been reduced to 1,390 km (864 miles) for the standard gauge and 63 km (39 miles) for the narrow gauge, which is being converted to mixed gauge. Another short narrow-gauge line, from Nanu Oya to Ragalla in the mountains, has closed.

However, in 1991, an extension of the broad gauge for 121 km (75 miles) from Matara to the pilgrim town of Kataragam on the south coast was begun, and there are proposals to extend this into the mountains to join up with Badulla, the railhead beyond Kandy and Nuwara Eliya. An 11 km (7 mile) branch from Anuadhapura to Mihintale in the north was due for completion in 1997.

Steam traction was the mainstay of the railways until the 1970s. By then the high cost of imported coal had led to the early development of British-built diesel traction, both locomotives and DMUs, an attractively styled version of which worked the frequent local services along the pictureque coastline from Colombo to the resort of Mount Lavinia. Japanese-built DMUs bought in 1990 now operate the local services.

Colombo's main railway station is at Fort and is a "through" station. Five platforms served the broad gauge and there was one for the narrow gauge. It always was busy, but suburban traffic has

● **LEFT**
Another less technically advanced form of transport in rural Sri Lanka is the ox cart.

INFORMATION BOX

Termini	Colombo and Kandy
Country	Sri Lanka
Distance	121 km (75 miles)
Date of opening	1868

increased by 30 per cent since 1980. Just to the north of Fort lies the important station of Maradana, with no fewer than six platform faces for the broad gauge and three for the narrow. It is the junction where the narrow gauge heads off down the Kelani valley. About 1.2 km (3/4 mile) further on, the large locomotive depot and repair shops at Dermatagoda at the right of the line provided eight long tracks for broad-gauge and two for narrow-gauge locomotives. This was by far the largest depot on the island and, for such a relatively small system, the

● **OPPOSITE TOP**
Colombo's House of Assembly, the seat of Sri Lanka's parliament.

● **OPPOSITE MIDDLE**
This railcar, No. 331 of Class V2, operated on the 2 ft 6 in gauge lines.

● **BELOW LEFT**
There were four batches of Class B8c dating back to 1922. Two of the batches were built by Hunslet Engine Co. of Leeds, England, and this machine was from the batch delivered in 1927. With an axle load of only 9.2 tonnes (9 tons), they were suitable for use on lightly laid track.

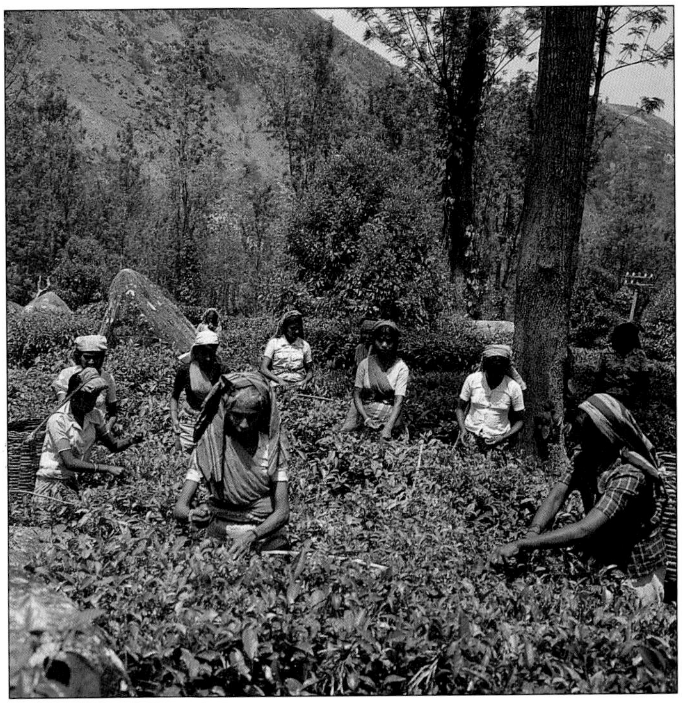

● **OPPOSITE BOTTOM**
The 2 ft 6 in gauge line from Colombo up the Kelani valley saw locomotives such as this neat J1 Class 2-6-2T No. 220.

● **RIGHT**
A familiar sight by the side of the line in Sri Lanka are the tea pickers working in the plantations.

● LEFT
Another familiar sight by the side of the line in Sri Lanka are the rice paddy fields.

the mainland of the Indian subcontinent. It is also the end of the double-track section, and the train for Kandy turns away to the east, gently climbing to Rambukkana, 11 km (7 miles) further on at a height of 95 m (312 ft).

The 29 km (18 mile) section from Rambukkana to Peradenya is one of the most spectacular in Sri Lanka. Travellers are advised to sit on the right-hand side of the train to take advantage of the ever-changing scene. A large 4-8-0 banking locomotive of Class A1 is placed at the rear of the train to assist on the 19 km (12 mile) climb at 1:44, made more difficult by numerous sharp curves down to 201 m (660 ft) radius.

The route leaves the jungle floor and climbs on ledges frequently cut from the almost vertical rock faces. The expanding

number of different types of locomotive that had to be maintained, ranging from diminutive narrow-gauge 4-4-0T to Beyer-Garratts, must have put a strain on the skills and resources of the engineers.

The double-track main line generally heads north-east through level countryside with paddy fields, coconut plantations and small villages with palm-thatched huts. Areas of uncultivated land are often ablaze with the blooms of wild flowers, and brightly coloured birds complete the scene. At Ragama, the branch line along the west coast to Puttalam goes off to the left.

By Ambepussa, 56 km (35 miles) from Colombo, the train has begun to climb away from the wide coastal plains through coconut plantations until its arrival at Polgahawela, 74 km (46 miles) from Colombo at an altitude of 73 m (240 ft) above sea level. This is the junction for the main line northward, which finishes at Kankesanturai, where there is a ferry to

● RIGHT
Class B1a 4-6-0 Sir Thomas Maitland was built in England in 1927 by Beyer Peacock and is seen in a much more colourful livery than that used in 1945.

● RIGHT
Class B2c 4-6-0 No. 213 is one of several engines delivered from 1915 onward and comes from a batch manufactured by Vulcan Foundry in England in 1922. It is essentially a main-line locomotive, and, until the arrival of Class B1, it was the pride of the line.

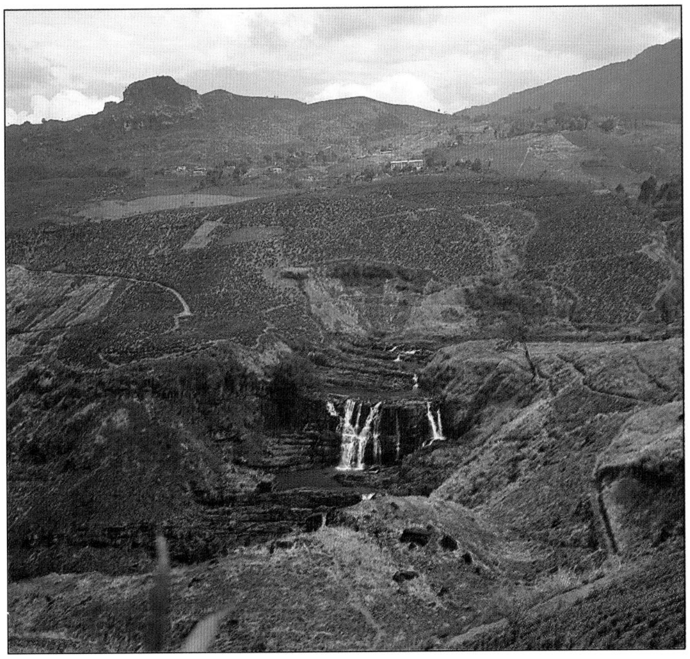

● LEFT
A typical scene in Sri Lanka's hill country.

● ABOVE
The Class B10 4-6-0 had the very light axle load of only 7.6 tonnes (7.5 tons) enabling it to work over lightly laid lines such as that to Matale. The class dates back to 1901.

views, first into the valley below and then into the far distance, are incomparable. "Sensation Curve" is rightly named for it is on a ledge with a 305 m (1,000 ft) sheer drop to the valley floor below. It is best seen from a train going toward Colombo, for it then appears that the line is going to take off into space.

Kadugannawa, 104 km (65 miles) from Colombo and 515 m (1,690 ft) above sea level, is where the banking locomotive is removed. The line then falls 41 m (136 ft) in the 9.6 km (6 miles) to Peradeniya Junction station, where the route to Newara Eliya and Badulla turns south while the other line turns north-east for the 6.4 km (4 miles) to Kandy. It is well worth pausing at New Peradeniya station to visit the nearby Botanical Gardens and wander through the extensive grounds.

The station at Kandy, 121 km (75 miles) from Colombo, had three terminal roads and one which continued through the station to Matale, 26 km (16 miles) distant and a centre for the cattle trade. Lightweight 4-6-0 steam locomotives were shedded here, together with two Sentinel Steam coaches, which worked local trains to Matale and Peradeniya.

● BELOW
Travellers will want to take time off in Kandy to visit the world-famous Temple of the Tooth. Here we see the temple across the lake of the same name.

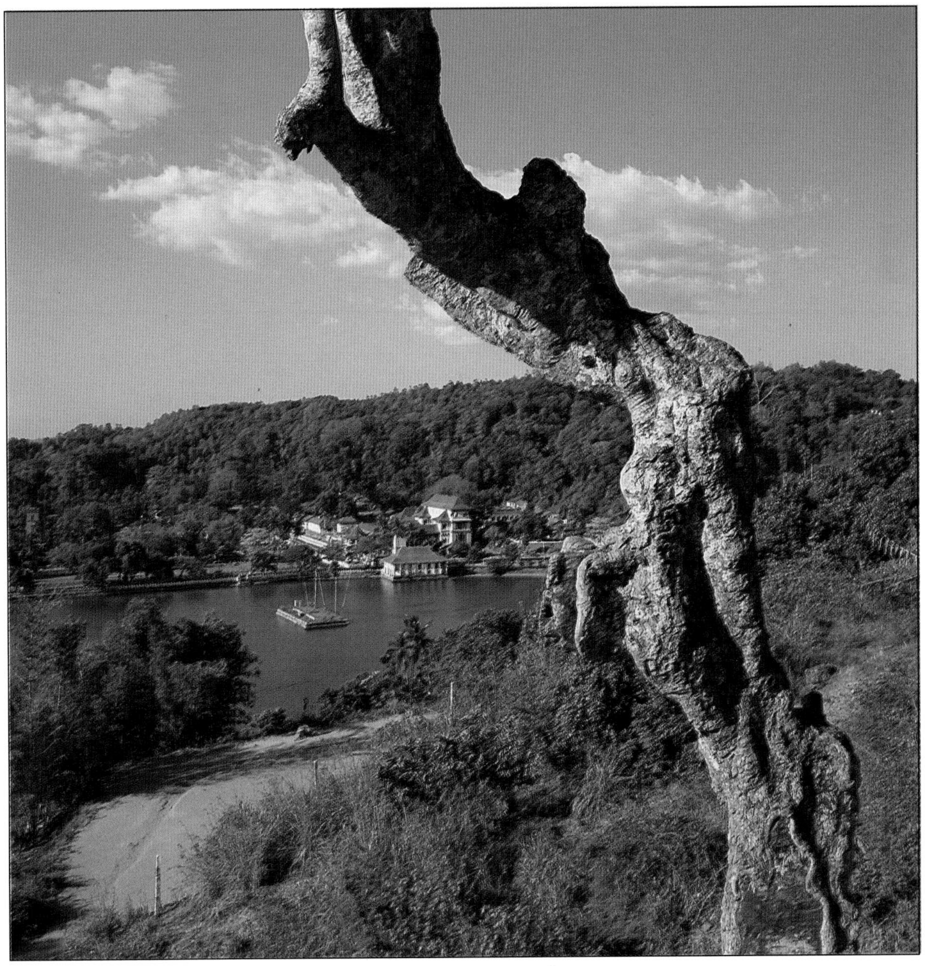

Tumenjan to Pyongyang

● LEFT
One of the freight-yard working steam locomotives at Nampo station.

"What do you want to go *there* for?" exclaimed the Russian engine-driver in amazement. "Don't you know there are *Communists* there?" He made it sound as if Russia had never had anything to do with Communism itself.

I was ensconced in the cab of the leading heavy diesel unit of the two deemed necessary to haul one battered coach along the single-track line that runs southwards from Ussuriysk, the junction for Vladivostok, the city of which could be seen in the distance, to Pyongyang, the capital of North Korea. There were no more than half a dozen passengers on the train, and, beyond Ussuriysk and the eyes of authority, I was actually permitted to drive the train as far as Khazan, border town of the then USSR, China and North Korea. At this politically sensitive spot, it was deemed prudent for me to return to the carriage.

Tumenjan is the North Korean entry station on this remote line, and the red banners and giant portraits of the "Great Leader" proclaimed entry into the hard-line Stalinist state where such propaganda drips from every village, town and city wall – even some of the mountain flanks.

INFORMATION BOX

Termini	Tumenjan and Pyongyang
Country	North Korea
Distance	*c.* 800 km (500 miles)
Date of opening	1899

Pyongyang's main station is a cross between a cathedral and an opera house in a city risen from the ashes of the 1950–53 Korean War to resemble a metropolis straight out of a Jules Verne fantasy (with a metro outshining even the architectural magnificence of Moscow's). Regretably, the marbled platforms of the station are closed to the rank and file who have to wait for their trains outside in the open.

Korea, as a whole, first opened its railway in 1899, and a 6,400 km (3,977 mile) network was developed during the Japanese annexation between 1910 and 1945. At partition in 1948, the network

● LEFT
A general view of Pyongyang.

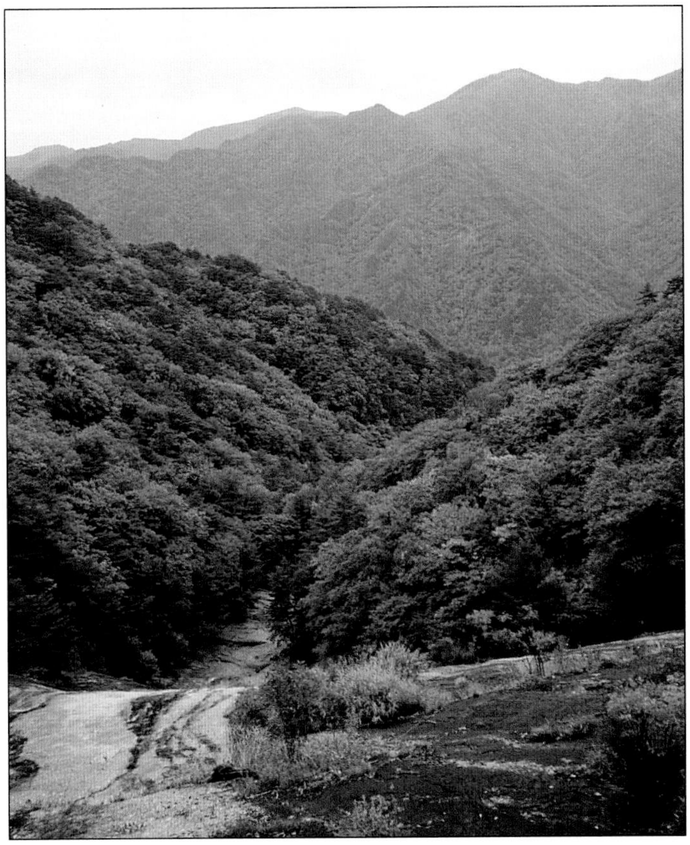

● RIGHT
Views of the North Korean mountains can be seen as the train travels through the countryside.

One of the towns served by the railway is Nampo, site of the 8 km (5 mile) long West Sea Barrage, a major engineering project of which North Korea is justly proud. It was here that I was allowed to ride in the cab of one of the freight-yard's working steam locomotives – the dirtiest I have seen for quite a long time. While some of the lines have been electrified in North Korea, the majority of trains are still diesel-hauled.

I left the country on the Pyongyang to Beijing express, crossing the Yalu River on the massive steel-lattice swing bridge into China's Manchuria, with far less rumpus than had one General Douglas MacArthur in the early 1950s.

and stock were divided on a ratio of 2:1, North Korea getting the greater share. The war destroyed much of the network, but this has now been rebuilt and improved upon – particularly in South Korea, which has outstripped in route-length its fractious neighbour.

As in all one-time Communist states, a permit is necessary for movement beyond a certain radius. This means that only those passengers engaged in labour for the State can travel worthwhile distances, which at least eliminates the scourge of overcrowded trains. Besides the line to Pyongyang from the Russian border, the only other lines run from the capital to the Chinese border at Dandong and southwards to Haeju and Kaesong, the town nearest the heavily fortified demarcation zone centred upon the village of Panmunjom (which, oddly, Western visitors are permitted to visit, albeit under guard, to stand just centimetres away from the actual line of demarcation separating the two halves of the country).

● LEFT AND BELOW
The North Korean–Russian border station of Tumenan.

SHENYANG TO HARBIN

The Chinese, in the midst of their modernization of the railways, are justifiably amused, not to say perplexed, that foreigners should want to travel thousands of miles to gape at their remaining steam-engines. Railway construction came late to Imperial China, forbidden (it is said) by successive emperors. By the 1880s, when the USA already possessed some 145,000 km (90,000 miles) of track, China had a mere 18,000 km (11,000 miles). However, once the ban was lifted the country took to railway construction with gusto. And no part of China is more rail-minded and enthusiastic about trains than Manchuria, a vast region, larger than France and Germany combined, that the Chinese call Dongbei.

Between 1876 and 1949, some 21,000 km (13,050 miles) of railway were built, though only half of it was operative following the civil war that led to the Communist take-over. Today's rail system exceeds 60,000 km (37,284 miles) with many single-track sections doubled.

It is in Manchuria, where there are huge deposits of brown coal, that steam traction can still be observed. Life on the Manchurian railways is often hard – in winter, when temperatures fall as low as –25°C (–13°F), locomotives can freeze to the rails. Yet even at such times earnest train buffs descend on the yards to take pictures with frost-affected cameras and enter copious notes into their pocket notebooks. In fact so many such visitors now arrive that today the workers are less mystified by all the attention.

The capital of Manchuria's Liaoning Province – one of three provinces – is Shenyang, the former Mukden. This is the scene of the "Mukden Incident", which arose when an explosion on the railway line triggered the Japanese occupation. Sixty km (37 miles) away, on a branch of the main Shenyang-Harbin line, sits the smaller city of Fushan, site of the prison, still operational, that held Pi Yi, the "Last Emperor", whose cell is open for inspection.

• TOP
A view of Harbin's vast marshalling yards from Sankong Bridge, with the city of Harbin in the background.

• ABOVE LEFT
Harbin railway station.

• LEFT
A China Railways QJ Class 2-10-2 storms up Wang Gang Bank out of Harbin with a heavy freight bound for Changchun.

INFORMATION BOX

Termini	Shenyang and Harbin
Country	China
Distance	*c.* 725 km (*c.* 450 miles)
Commencement of building	1876

For true rail buffs the Shenyang-Harbin line puts on a huge display of gigantic black steam locomotives, or at least it did in 1990. The route takes a full day to cover, and longer if one stops off to visit the sheds, where visitors are welcome.

The line was once the so-called Russian Manchurian Railway, and there is much in Harbin to remind one of the long gone Russian occupation. Between the small towns of Lungxiang and Lancha, about five hours' ride from Harbin, a narrow-gauge railway, using fussy little steam-engines, transports both visitors and timber between forest and town. On the main line the long-distance trains are adequate rather than luxurious, but at the railway towns *en route* the workers in the sidings and sheds are the friendliest imaginable, much heartened by the interest shown by visitors.

Harbin railway station is the third largest in China, with an average daily departure of over 200,000 passengers. With a floor space of 14,200 sq m (152,848 sq ft), it contains five waiting rooms, 28 booking offices, a restaurant, a department store, a left-luggage office and a hotel with over 300 beds.

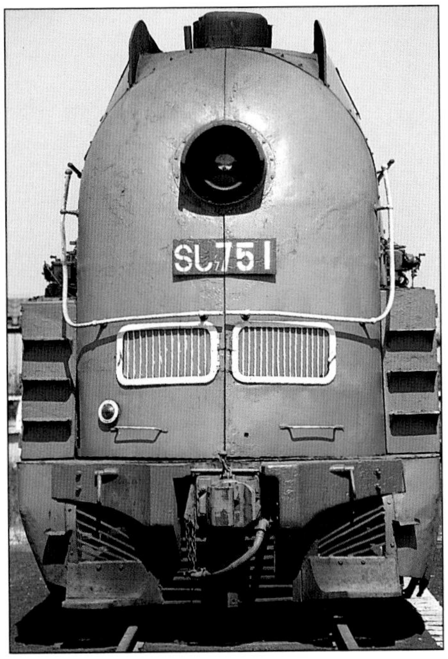

● **ABOVE**
One of the magnificent Japanese-built streamlined Pacifics in the Railway Museum at Shenyang. During the 1930s these engines worked the Asia Express between Shenyang – then known as Mukden – and Harbin.

● **ABOVE**
The city of Anshan, China's iron and steel capital, shows a wonderful diversity of architectures combined with the landscaped parks in which China excels.

● **LEFT**
A QJ Class 2-10-2 races down Wang Gang Bank and into Harbin on a frozen afternoon.

● **LEFT**
In China public transport is practised to a fine art as the private motor car barely exists. The back-up for China's excellent public transport system is the humble bicycle, and bike jams are a regular feature of rush-hour travel.

Ulan Bator to Datong Across the Gobi Desert

• BELOW
Serenity may be found in the country's only functioning Buddhist temple.

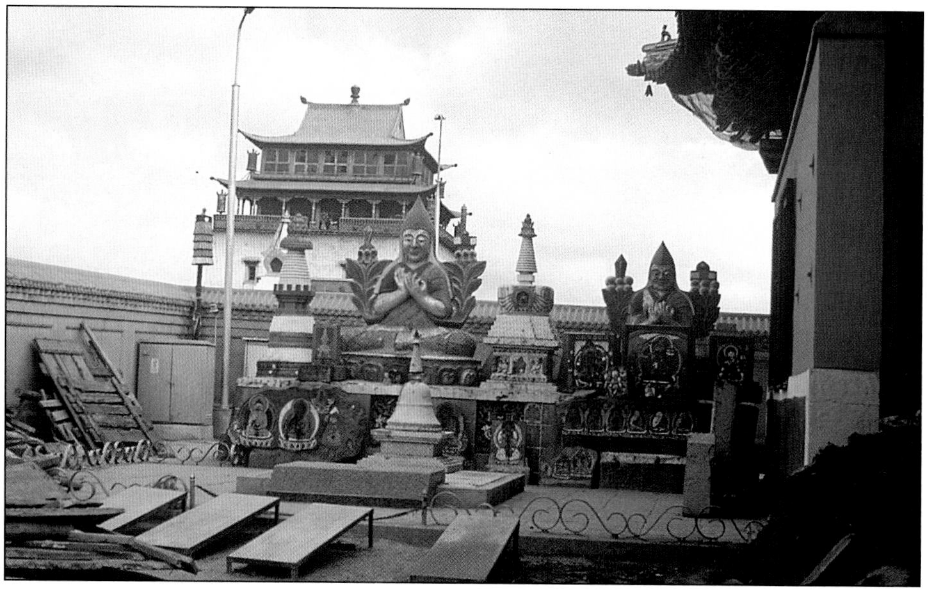

The train out of Ulan Bator, made up of seven coaches plus a baggage car, is normally in pristine condition. Before departure, all the coaches are given a final clean by smartly dressed attendants. Inside the four-berth coaches, the upper berths make up as beds, while there is plenty of room to sit on the lower seats, each covered by an attractive clean cloth.

On leaving Ulan Bator, the views are at first rather uninspiring. There is a confusing mixture of austere housing, steam-draped heavy industry and *yurts* (tents) against a backdrop of low hills. Items of railway interest include an ancient working 2.8.0 steam locomotive, a preserved industrial or narrow-gauge engine and some 20 diesels. Once having left the capital behind, the train winds through a sparse landscape, with almost bare hills to the left and occasional clumps of forest on the right.

About half an hour into the journey, the train loops around a set of three aerials as it climbs on to a flat plateau. An hour or so later it encounters an almost volcanic outcropping, before curving left and accelerating down a gentle downgrade. The train now traverses a seemingly endless hot flat plain until it reaches Choyr, where the landscape falls away gently to the right.

There are subtle changes in the terrain over the next couple of hours. A jagged rocky ridge in the left middle distance glows purple in the sunlight while the plain becomes gently undulating with dried grass and light soil on either side. The sinuous nature of the route, despite the level landscape, allows frequent views of the twin diesels, which haul the train, relatively slowly, through almost mesmeric terrain.

On the border, the Mongolian officials are all very smart and correct. A number of soldiers stand to attention along the platform. Formalities last between 23.40 and 01.00, and then the train is on the move once again, this time entering China or, to be pedantic, Chinese-dominated Inner Mongolia.

The welcome at the first Chinese station is very different from the arrivals experienced in the once-Soviet sphere of influence. The station is festooned with coloured lights, and cheerful music is relayed from loud-speakers, all in marked

INFORMATION BOX

Termini	Ulan Bator and Datong
Countries	Mongolia and China
Distance	1045 km (655 miles)
Date of opening	1929

• BELOW
A QJ Class 2-10-2 and a JS Class 2-8-2 are subjects of interest at an intermediate station.

● **RIGHT**
Impressive public buildings and lesser structures stretch towards the foothills beyond Ulan Bator.

● **BELOW RIGHT**
A carving of Buddha in the Yungang gorge.

contrast to both the desert and other more drab administrations encountered previously. The formalities can still be lengthy, nevertheless, and some passengers may miss the experience of seeing the train being converted to run on the Chinese gauge.

The line from Ulan Bator to Datong was built by the Soviets to their broader gauge of 5 ft but, following the cooling of relations between them and China, the Chinese re-laid their portion of the route to the local (standard) gauge, viz. 1,435 4 ft 8½ in. This need to change gauge gives the traveller the first opportunity to travel behind steam. The locomotive hauls the train about 1. 6 km (1 mile) to the shed equipped to change bogies.

Apart from the engine crew, nearly all the workers engaged in the operation are female. The locomotive positioned, each coach opposite a pair of jacks, preparations are made to the bogies and the brake gear. Then the coach is jacked up, the bogies are rolled away, to be replaced by a new set by overhead crane. Finally the coach is lowered and fine adjustments, if necessary, are made to the position of the new bogies. Regular practice has, however, made the initial positioning of both coach and wheelsets remarkably accurate. Once everything is correctly positioned, and the requisite connections have been made, the whole process is repeated for the next coach.

During breakfast on the second day the views of isolated forts and ruined walls on the passing heights – remnants of the defences of the Great Wall – remind travellers that they are entering China proper. The train follows a winding river valley, as doubtless earlier invaders would have done. They, however, would not have encountered increasing signs of industrialization as the train appraoches Datong. Pollution control is still a relatively foreign concept, and the fumes from the various factories, mingled with the smell of night-soil in the more rural areas, make for a potent mixture.

A succession of passing steam-hauled freights provides evidence not only of industry but also of how effective the distribution system of the Chinese is compared with that of the Russians. Water melons, pears, apples, plums, grapes, cabbages, peppers, beetroot, swede, carrots and chillies are all visible on the trains and for sale in these northern regions in contrast to the former Soviet Union. A journey across the Gobi Desert in many ways remains one in time as well as kilometres.

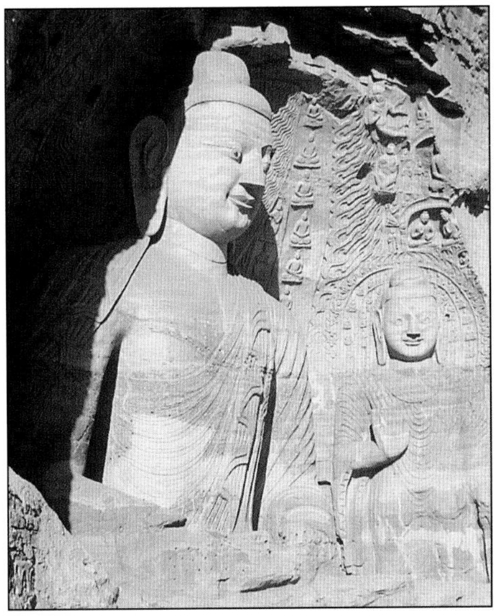

● **BELOW**
The train sweeps round a sun-baked village, the passengers probably oblivious to the harsh life of its inhabitants.

Fuji to Kofu

● LEFT
Interior of a JR EMU assigned to the Fujikawa express trains. This train was the Fujikawa No. 5, heading to Kofu from Fuji.

A pleasant one-day jaunt from Tokyo is to ride on the metre-gauge Minobu line, which runs from the city of Fuji, near the base of the famous Mount Fuji, to Kofu. A circular trip from Tokyo via Fuji and Kofu is easily accomplished with a little planning. Fuji is served by both the Tokyo-Osaka-Hakata Shinkansen high-speed line (also known as the Tokaido-San-Yo Shinkansen) and the metre-gauge Tokaido line of Japanese Railways (JR). Trains operating on the Minobu line use the same station as the Tokaido line, and passengers can make a cross-the-platform transfer here. The Shinkansen Shin-Fuji station is several blocks distant from the metre-gauge station, making transfer between trains more difficult.

The northern end of the Minobu line joins JR's busy metre-gauge Chou Line a mile east of the main station in Kofu, where another cross-the-platform transfer takes place. There is frequent and direct service to Tokyo on this incredibly scenic main line, and a number of interesting streamlined trains run this way, including the Super Azusa and the Boso View – which despite its name is not a circus train!

Fuji is an industrial city on Suruga Bay and warrants a considerable volume of freight service on the Tokaido line in addition to frequent passenger service. While making a connection to the Minobu line, passengers may see one of many intermodal freights pass through the station or watch a diesel hydraulic-switch engine shunt cars in the nearby yard.

● ABOVE LEFT
After a five-minute stop at Minobu, a local train's conductor checks his watch before departing for Kofu. Most of the Minobu line is single track with passing sidings at key stations. Local trains are required to clear the way for Fujikawa expresses.

● LEFT
A Fujikawa express train races through Hadakajima on its way to Fuji. The Minobu line passes through fabulous mountainous terrain on its run between Fuji and Kofu.

● LEFT
A local train, bound for Fuji from Kofu, coasts downgrade toward its station stop at Hadakajima.

INFORMATION BOX

Termini	Fuji and Kofu
Country	Japan
Distance	97 km (60 miles)
Date of opening	Information unavailable

There are both local and express trains on the Minobu line. Local trains are usually equipped with JR's Spartan but very clean electric multiple units (EMUs) of the sort found in commuter service all around Japan. The seating is not of the best sort for a long trip, but the windows are clean. Express service is provided by considerably more luxurious multiple-unit trains, which run as the Fujikawa. A JR Green Pass will entitle foreign visitors to travel on these express trains; otherwise first-class tickets can be purchased from JR. The Fujikawa operates on a significantly faster schedule than the local trains; it attains a top speed of 85 kph (53 mph), and stops much less often, making the Fuji-Kofu run in just under two hours. Local trains can take a little more than three hours to cover the same distance.

Leaving Fuji, the Minobu line follows the Urui River and winds through residential neighbourhoods and industrial areas of the city. In addition to the local through trains, commuter trains also serve suburban Fuji on the lower end of the line. On a clear day, Mount Fuji is visible to the north of the tracks. Several miles out of town, the railroad leaves the Urui and follows the Fujikawa River, one of the most important waterways in Japan. On the way up the scenic Fujikawa valley, the railroad passes through many short tunnels and provincial towns. The line is primarily single track, with short passing sidings at most stations allowing for well-timed meets between opposing trains. Towards Kofu the railroad drops down into a broad agricultural plain.

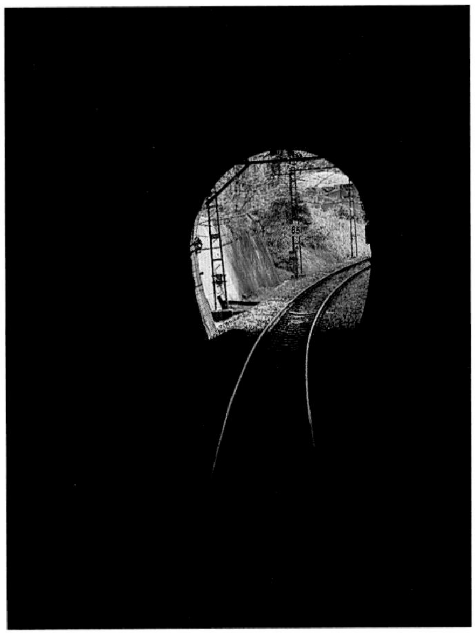

● ABOVE
The Minobu line features many tunnels, including several long bores near Wariishi Pass, located between Shimobe and Kofu.

● LEFT
A Super Azusa train departs the Kofu terminal for Tokyo via the Chou line. Upon arriving at Kofu from Fuji, passengers may continue on to Tokyo on a number of interesting streamlined electric trains, including the Super Azusa.

Tokyo's Yamanote Line

BELOW
A Yamanote line train leaves Shinjuku.

The Yamanote line makes a 32 km (20 mile) loop through Tokyo, connecting the city's principal rail terminals at Shinjuku, Ueno and Tokyo stations. Other lines operate immediately parallel to this extremely busy metre-gauge electrified commuter line, including the busy Tokaido, Chou, and Seibu-Shinjuku lines, making the Yamanote Loop route one of the busiest railway lines in the world. In many places, the right of way has between six and twelve main-line tracks.

Many long-distance trains, including Japanese Railway's (JR's) overnight sleeping car trains, run alongside the Yamanote commuters. Riding the loop, one might even see one of the new streamlined silver and purple Super Azusa trains pacing your train on an adjacent track! Service on the Yamanote line itself is provided by JR EMU commuter train sets painted light green (all of the Tokyo area commuter train routes are colour-coded) that run around the loop continuously. The trains run every couple of minutes between 6 a.m. and midnight.

INFORMATION BOX

Termini	Shinjuku, Ueno and Tokyo
Country	Japan
Distance	32 km (20 miles)
Date of opening	Information unavailable

FAR LEFT
At Shinjuku, on a platform adjacent to the Yamanote line, is one of JR's new Super Azusa train sets. Soon this metre-gauge streamliner will head out on the Chou line towards Kofu.

OPPOSITE BOTTOM
A long Yamanote line train departs Habata station in the morning rush hour. These trains run on one- and two-minute headways at peak times, and are nearly always jam-packed right up to midnight.

● LEFT
The Shinjuku shopping district on a sunny weekday morning is a primary destination of many railway commuters. The Shinjuku region of Tokyo is served by many railway lines including the busy Yamanote line.

At Akihabara the Sobu line crosses the Yamanote line on an exceptionally tall elevated structure, with the Sobu line on the upper level. Far below one can observe the Shinkansen. Akihabara is known as "Electric City", and the latest electronic devices imaginable are available here, from electric toilet seats to singing alarm clocks!

Although the Yamanote line is run by JR as part of the commuter rail network, the level and quality of service resembles a rapid transit line more than that of a conventional commuter train line.

Most of the line is either elevated or depressed through Tokyo, offering many excellent views of the city. However, the Yamanote line's principal attraction is the astounding volume of rail traffic along this route. Shinjuku station on the west side of Tokyo presently ranks as the world's busiest railroad station, including two interurban electric terminals adjacent to it. At rush hour, on any week day, traffic through this terminal is virtually continuous.

At Ueno, a 12-track flying junction separates metre-gauge routes on to two levels. (The Shinkansen is below ground at this point.) It is not uncommon to find six trains moving in different directions through Ueno all at one time! Ueno station serves Ueno Park, the location of several museums and the Tokyo Zoo. The Tokyo Science Museum is only a block from Ueno station and features a preserved JR 2-8-2 Mikado-type steam locomotive and a semaphore signal.

The Shinkansen runs alongside the Yamanote Loop at several places on the east side of Tokyo. At traffic peaks these high-speed trains operate every five or six minutes, yet traffic on the parallel metre-gauge line is even more frequent.

● RIGHT
Ueno station in Tokyo, one of several large busy stations connected on the Yamanote line.

TOKYO TO NIKKO
BY TRAIN TO THE SHRINES

It is a cliché to state that Japan is a land of contrasts, but anyone visiting the country cannot help but come to that conclusion. A visit by train to Nikko is one of the many ways of experiencing this. Nikko is one of the major Japanese temple and shrine areas and, at approximately 150 km (93 miles) from Tokyo, is the nearest to the capital. The contrast is not only between the city noise and the calm of the temples, but also between the express train on the Tobu Railway, the Japanese Railways (JR) semi-rural branch line and a trip on the "Bullet train" (Shinkansen).

● LEFT
Tobu Railway Spacia EMU 102-6 at Nikko. The streamlined styling is more for appearance than practical benefit, given the relatively low speeds reached.

The round trip starts at Asakusa station in Tokyo. The area around the station, close to the Sumida River, is itself worth visiting, with its large number of craft goods shops and the large Sensoji Temple. This elevated station, integrated into the second floor of the Matsuya department store and at the end of a bridge over the river, is the terminus of the Tobu Railway. The site is very cramped, and many of their trains now run through to the Eidan Hibiya metro line from a junction around 10 km (6 miles) out of town. There are only three six-coach platforms, and plans for a total rebuild are under discussion, not least to allow the Tobu's standard ten-coach

● ABOVE
Tokyo has two metro systems, a "private" company, TRTA, and the city authority's TOEI group. This is TRTA metro 05014 at Nakano, on the Tozai line. Asakusa station is served by the TRTA Ginza line.

● LEFT
Tobu Railway Spacia EMU departing Asakusa station, Tokyo, in December 1995. Note the curved approach to the station from the river bridge, on the right of the photograph.

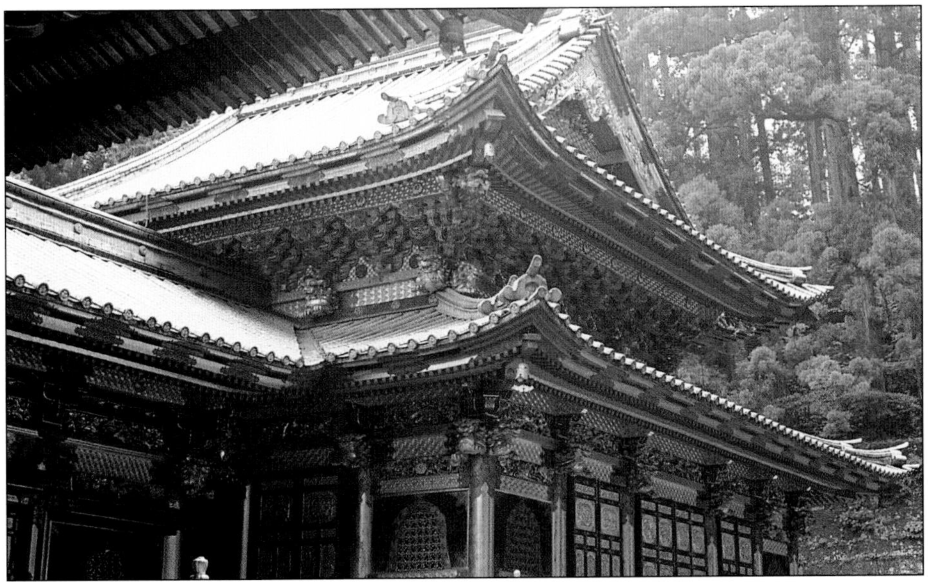

● LEFT
Detail on the buildings at the Daiyuin Shrine. The proximity of the forest can be seen in the background.

● BELOW
Tobu Railway EMU 6267 arriving in Nikko.

● BOTTOM
JR's Nikko station building. The small garden cum shrine on the left is fairly typical. Note the JR practice of including the romanized version of place-names on the station name-boards.

trains to use the station.

Nikko can be reached on the suburban trains, but the quicker and definitely more comfortable way is to travel on one of the Tobu's "Limited Express Spacia" trains, which are formed of streamlined EMUs. There are six through trains in the morning, taking an hour and 40 minutes, followed by a half-hourly service for most of the day, requiring one change at Shimo Imaichi. The Spacia trains come complete with hostess and drinks service, and the seats are a pleasant contrast to the longitudinal seats on the suburban trains.

The Asakusa ticket-office can be confusing to those who do not speak Japanese, but a little observation will identify the special queue for these trains. Seat reservation is compulsory, but can be bought on the day, and there should not be too many problems getting a place

INFORMATION BOX

Termini	Tokyo and Nikko
Country	Japan
Distance	150 km (93 miles)
Date of opening	Infomation unavailable

● LEFT
JR outer-suburban EMU 115-422 and JR freight electric locomotive EF65 540 at Utsunomiya. The Tohoku Shinkansen platforms are in the structure above the platform on the left.

on the next departure. Sign language is adequate to buy a ticket!

The main line of the Tobu Railway was built in the first decade of this century, and Nikko was reached in 1929 at a time of electrification and expansion. The present Asakusa terminus was opened in 1931. Through running of Tobu trains to the Tokyo metro, starting in 1962, was the first of its kind in Tokyo. The Tobu Railway is one of the largest private railways in Japan and carried over 945 million passengers on 463 km (288 miles) of route during 1994, totalling over four billion passenger kilometres (2.5 billion miles). Unlike commuter railways in other countries, but like most in Japan, the Tobu Railway is profitable, despite its cheap fares.

The line proceeds through the ever-expanding suburban sprawl of Tokyo for some time but eventually reaches the country area beyond. The landscape is attractive rather than dramatic, with the low hills, woods and paddy fields interspersed with farm buildings and small towns. However, as the journey progresses, mountains come into view. Whilst the railway does not reach them, the mountains form a backdrop to the area around Nikko, with three peaks over 2,000 m (6,500 ft) within 20 km (12 miles) of the town.

There are no great engineering features on the line caused by the terrain. However, in order to avoid frequent level crossings and to expand capacity in its evolution from a local line into a four-track commuter railway, significant stretches of elevated line have been constructed, on ugly concrete structures.

The Tobu station in Nikko is the closest to the town centre, although the JR station is only 200 m (650 ft) further away. The shrines are about 2 km

● BELOW
JR's Utsunomiya station. On the left is the Nikko branch train formed of EMU 106-7. On the right is outer-suburban EMU 115-122.

● RIGHT
The Shinkyo bridge, Nikko, a 1907 reconstruction of a 17th-century original. This can be seen from the road between Nikko and the shrine area.

● BELOW RIGHT
The "three wise monkeys" carving on the sacred stables at the Toshogu Shrine.

(1¼ miles) from the railway stations, along a road lined with many shops aimed at the Japanese tourist market. The more adventurous could try some of the food shops, most of which make few compromises for the non-Japanese. There is also a bus service.

Around half-way along the road is the Nikko Information Centre, which is also the main outlet for the cheapest way to visit the temples: the two-shrines-one-temple ticket. The ticket offices at the sites will try to sell you individual entry tickets, a far more expensive combination. The attendant in the office seemed surprised that a foreigner had found his way there and knew about this ticket. However, the information is given in any good guidebook, which will also help you understand the history behind this religious site.

The area contains (despite the name of the ticket!) four main attractions: the Rinnoji Temple, the Daiyuin Shrine, the Futarasan Shrine and the Toshogu Shrine. The latter contains the original of the "hear no evil, see no evil, speak no evil" carving and is the most visited. However, all four are recommended, and are listed in the suggested viewing order. The Toshogu Shrine, dating from 1617 and including a five-storey pagoda, is undoubtedly the most famous and, unfortunately, has the crowds to match. This contrasts with the Daiyuin Shrine, which few people seem to reach. All the buildings are set amongst a forest of tall trees, giving an appropriately serene atmosphere to a site with religious links going back to the 8th century.

The return journey starts with the JR branch line from Nikko to Utsunomiya, which opened in 1890. The service is frequent, if not entirely regular, and starts from a white, half-timbered building, which appears in style to be a cross between Japanese and English Victorian mock-Tudor architecture. The train usually consists of a suburban-style two-car EMU.

The first part of the 40-minute journey is through the countryside and small towns. The significant number of

● LEFT
The Senso-ji Temple complex includes the massive Hozomon Gate, seen here from the temple steps.

● BELOW LEFT
JR suburban EMU approaching Ueno Station, Tokyo. This train is on the upper level, the tracks visible on a lower level are used by long distance trains. The Shinkansen from Utsonomiya and the north is on a third, underground level at this station.

school students on my train showed that the railway was not just run for the visitors to Nikko. The scenery becomes more urban as Utsunomiya, a large town, is approached. Its station is in two adjoining parts: the main JR station and the elevated Shinkansen platforms. There is also a Tobu Railway terminus in the vicinity, also with services to Tokyo.

JR is now the poor relation on this route – although journey times are comparable, most people visiting Nikko now tend to use the Tobu line. However, JR did not give up without a fight, and the 1950s were characterized by the two companies vying to provide the best service and best rolling stock to gain the most passengers; by the mid-1960s, however, the Tobu had won.

The Shinkansen journey is on the Tohoku line, which runs between Tokyo and Morioka, to the north. Trains run from Utsunomiya to Tokyo approximately three times per hour and take around 55 minutes for approximately 108 km (67 miles). This journey will be taken using the unreserved seating on the Shinkansen, unless there was enough time to plan the schedule in detail a day or so in advance. The unreserved seats are only in specified coaches, and the ticket will indicate which. It is recommended to be near the front of the queue, which will be at exactly the right spot on the platform to be opposite the door when the train stops.

The Tohoku line opened north from the Tokyo suburban station of Omiya in 1982, 78 km (48 miles) from Utsunomiya, and reached Ueno in 1985; the final section into Tokyo being opened in 1991. The run to Tokyo is elevated for much of the way through largely built-up areas as far as Ueno, the main station on the north side of Tokyo. From here, the line is in tunnel to Tokyo station where, although meeting the Tokaido line Shinkansen, there is no end-on junction

as the power supplies and automatic signalling systems are different. There is also a big contrast between this station and Asakusa, where the journey started. However, whilst Tokyo station seems vast and very busy, it is not the busiest station in Japan, a distinction belonging to Tokyo's Shinjuku station.

This round trip, which provides something for those culturally minded as well as those interested in the railways, can be done comfortably in a day from Tokyo The relative cheapness of rail fares in Japan means the strong yen does not make the cost overly expensive. It should be noted that this itinerary is not sold as one ticket and rebooking will be required in Nikko, but my total lack of knowledge of Japanese did not prove a barrier to a fascinating day out.

- **ABOVE**
JR Shinkansen 221-204 arriving at Utsunomiya. The two central tracks allow non-stopping trains to overtake, a quite frequent occurrence which requires strict adherence to the timetable to avoid delays.

- **BELOW LEFT**
Close by the Tobu Railway's Asakusa station is the Senso-ji Temple. One of the buildings in the complex is this five-storey pagoda.

- **BELOW**
JR Shinkansen 221-25 at Tokyo, in the low-level platforms used by the Tohoku line. The green livery is unique to the Shinkansen on this route.

TOKYO TO OSAKA

● LEFT
The interior of an older Shinkansen train set of the sort now used on local trains.

● BOTTOM
A Tokyo-bound express races through Shizuoka.

Just after World War II, the Japanese proposed to build a straight line between Tokyo and Osaka that would allow trains to travel at 201 kph (125 mph). However, with the massive rebuilding that had to take place after the war, it was not until 1958 that an aerial survey of the route was made. The following year, within a week of Parliament approving the project, the ceremonial ground-breaking took place. In 1965, just 65 months later, the first full service between the two cities began.

To permit such high speed, the line was constructed so that no curve had a radius of less than 2.4 km ($1\frac{1}{2}$ miles). To avoid urban congestion and to minimize noise, the line is carried on viaducts with high parapet walls some 6.4 m (21 ft) above towns. There are no level crossings on the track, and valleys and estuaries are crossed on long viaducts. Where mountains block the way, no fewer than 66 tunnels, 12 of them over 2 km ($1\frac{1}{4}$ miles) long, have been driven through the rock. To make allowance for the aerodynamic effect of two trains passing at combined speeds of over 400 kph (250 mph), the distance between the nearest rails of opposing track in the tunnels has been increased from the standard 1.83 m (6 ft) to between 2.74 m (9 ft) and 2.89 m (9 ft 6 in). Because of the high speed, care also had to be taken when building the embankments to ensure that there was an adequate degree of compactness in the piled-up earth.

● BELOW
The fastest regularly scheduled train in the world is the 300 kph (186 mph) Nozomi 500, which makes one round trip from Osaka to Hakata daily. It is seen here stopping at Okayama on its eastbound run.

From 06.00 to 21.00, a Hikari (Lightning) train leaves Tokyo every 15 minutes and covers the 518 km (322 miles) in three hours and ten minutes – stopping only twice, at Nagoya and Kyoto – at an average speed of over 160 kph (100 mph). Each train consists of 16 cars and carries an average of 1,000 passengers per train.

Because of the tunnels and the high windows in the coaches, travellers do not get a chance to see much of the beautiful scenery the train passes. It is only when the line crosses the broad river valleys that they can appreciate the Japanese countryside and the distant mountains, including Mount Fuji, of which there are magnificent views.

Today the Tokyo-Osaka Shinkansen is the busiest of several Shinkansen routes, with trains departing Tokyo as often as

● RIGHT
A Tokyo-bound Nozomi train nears its destination. The wedge-shaped train sets are usually assigned to either the Nozomi or Hikari trains running between Tokyo, Osaka and Hakata.

INFORMATION BOX

Termini	Tokyo and Osaka
Country	Japan
Length	518 km (322 miles)
Date of opening	1965

every six minutes at peak travel times. West of Osaka, the Shinkansen extends to Kobe, Okayama, Hiroshima and, by way of an undersea tunnel, to Hakata in the island of Kyushu. (The extension to Okayama opened in 1972, and to Hakata in 1975.) North of Tokyo, the Shinkansen extends to Niigata, Yamagata, Sendai and Morioka on separate routes. (The Morioka line opened in 1982.) Tokyo is the terminal for all lines, and there are no through trains between the western and eastern Shinkansen lines. However, there are regular express trains from Tokyo all the way to Hakata on the Osaka line.

Service is provided by three classes of trains: Kodama local trains, which make freqent stops; Hikari limited-express trains; and Nozomi extra-fare super-express trains. On the Tokyo-Osaka segment, there are now three generations of equipment in service, the newest dating from the early 1990s. The latest equipment is used for the Nozomi service. In March 1997 the Nozomi 500 entered service between Osaka and Hakata. This unmistakable train regularly operates at speeds of up to 300 kph (186 mph) and is now the fastest regularly scheduled train in the world. North of Tokyo, there is a pot-pourri of new train styles in service, including the double-deck "Max" trains.

● LEFT
One of the older Shinkansen train sets pauses to pick up passengers at Shizuoka. Many of these traditional "Bullet Trains" are now used as locals – albeit high-speed ones – while the newer equipment handles more glamorous Hikari and Nozomi express duties.

● BELOW
On a rainy April evening, two express trains pass at speed, while a local makes a station stop at Shizuoka. Service on the Tokyo-Osaka line is fast and frequent.

SINGAPORE TO BANGKOK
THE EASTERN AND ORIENTAL EXPRESS

The Eastern and Oriental (E&O) Express links Singapore, Kuala Lumpur and Bangkok. This luxury train started in 1993 and was the creation of James B. Sherwood, the owner of the Venice Simplon-Orient Express.

It is the world's first sleeping car train with a private shower and toilet in every cabin. The train consists of six standard double-bunk sleepers, seven State twin-bed sleepers and one Presidential double-bed sleeper with dressing-room. The whole totals 132 beds and is air-conditioned throughout with three dining cars, two service cars, a generator car, a bar car and an open-end observation car from which one can smell the jungle and hear the birds and the croaking frogs. The 22 cars are 433 m (1,421 ft) long and weigh 844 tons.

Built in Japan for the New Zealand Railways, the train is wholly redesigned by Frenchman Gérard Gallet, whose

INFORMATION BOX

THE EASTERN AND ORIENTAL EXPRESS	
Termini	Singapore and Bangkok
Countries	Malaysia and Thailand
Distance	1,943 km (1,207 miles)
Date built	1909–18

VSOE-type rounded brass handles protect sharp angles in the bar car, with its pale ash panelling, lotus motif décor and clever mirrors. Here the piano tinkles, two fortune tellers attend and the tireless, helpful Thai staff serve drinks late into the night.

In the cabins, the genuine welcome of the Thai personal staff, the elegant diamond-patterned parquetry, set off with antique brass fittings, all convey a highly civilized atmosphere to the guests. On leaving Singapore, afternoon tea is served, British Straits Settlements style. The sumptuous dining cars offer innovative Eurasian menus with fine wines. The brass torch and Pullman table lamps set off the lacquered Chinese or rare veneer panels, sparkling French glasses and gleaming silverware.

After passing customs at Singapore's Kappel station, the E&O enters Malaysia

• ABOVE LEFT
The observation car of the Eastern and Oriental Express, where passengers can admire the outstanding scenery alongside the track.

• LEFT
The Eastern and Oriental Express near Kanchanaburi, Thailand.

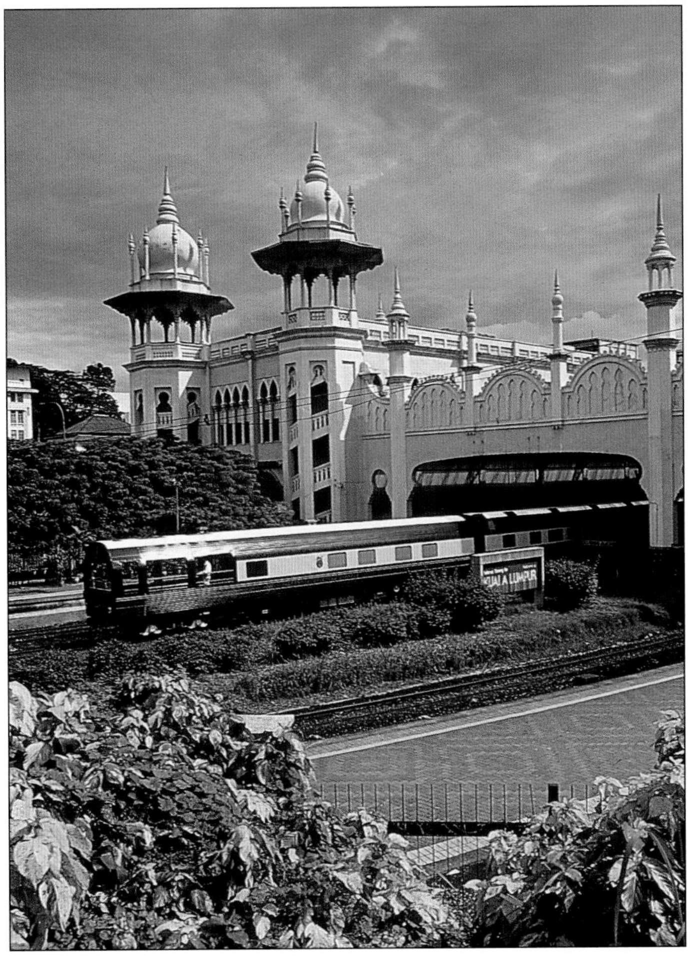

● **RIGHT**
The Eastern and Oriental Express at Kuala Lumpur's magnificent station.

● **FAR RIGHT**
The Eastern and Oriental Express crossing the 800 m (2,624 ft) long bridge over the River Kwai. This multi-span steel girder bridge spans on stone pillars approximately 4.5 m (15 ft) above the water.

● **BELOW RIGHT**
The Eastern and Oriental Express crossing the South East Asian countryside.

over the 6 km ($3^3/_4$ mile) long Johor Bahru causeway. Thereafter, as many have already experienced, the train makes a leisurely, varied journey on narrow-gauge tracks through the Malayan rubber plantations and primitive jungle, and later through Thailand's terraced farmlands, dotted with Buddhist shrines.

The train reaches Kuala Lumpur, 394 km (245 miles) from Singapore – and the world's most beautiful station – one hour before midnight. From now on, the line is on single track and the jungle closes in. After luncheon on the second day, the scene begins to change as Karst Limestone mountains rise from the lush plains near Padang Besar, where the Keretapi Tanah Malayu Railways (KTM) hand over to the State Railways of Thailand (SRT). On a historical foot-note, KTM first ran air-conditioned sleeping cars from Butterworth to Bangkok as early as 1936.

The next morning, after passing through Thai terraced farmlands during the night, the train stops on the east coast at Hua Hin. It is here that the Thai royal family spend their holidays, and the station is magnificent, with its royal waiting-room flanked by topiary in the form of elephants. Fresh supplies are brought aboard here. Later, near Nakhon Pathom, the express diverts some 70 km (43 miles) to visit the infamous bridge over the River Kwai.

Forty-two hours after leaving Singapore, having travelled 1,943 km (1,207 miles), the train arrives at Bangkok's Hualampong station. Most passengers end their journey here, but it is possible to spend a third night aboard by continuing 751 km (467 miles) north to Chiang Mai.

SINGAPORE TO PENANG

Although the description of this journey has been compiled from notes made on several runs in 1946 when overall timings were low, it is described as if made on one occasion. Fortunately, the whole journey is still possible today, and long may it remain so.

On the day of departure, the "Day Mail" to Kuala Lumpur left from Singapore station at 07.00, not long after dawn. The station at Tanjong Pagar, somewhat out of the centre of the city, was built in 1932 in the European style of the day. At the time of writing, it is still in use and has an impressive high-ceilinged entrance hall with three storeys of offices on one side and a restaurant and hotel on the other. Murals in painted tiles depict scenes on the railway.

The train comprised 12 coaches and two vans and was hauled by a Class 564 Pacific built in 1945. The author's coach

was built in 1935 and rode very well. After departing on time, and the fireman having collected the single-line token from the signalman, the train swung round past the locomotive and carriage sheds at the right. On a siding were small 0-4-0 tank locomotives belonging to the Singapore Harbour Board awaiting disposal. An 0-6-0T of the Federated Malayan States Railway (FMSR), which had been bought to replace them, was on shed together with a couple of MacArthur 2-8-2s, still bearing their

● TOP
A MacArthur Class WD10G4 drawing a train out of the carriage shed at Singapore in March 1946.

● ABOVE LEFT
The trolley bus was popular in Singapore and Penang. This one, built between the two world wars and pictured in December 1946, is on a service in Georgetown, capital of the island of Penang.

● LEFT
On the journey, the traveller passes many villages of which this is typical.

● **LEFT**
Kuala Lumpur's ornate railway station.

● **BELOW**
The signboard outside the funicular railway station on Penang Island gives an indication of the height of the mountains, whose relatively cool climate provides a welcome escape from the heat and humidity of Georgetown.

● **BOTTOM LEFT**
View from the summit station on the Swiss-built funicular on Penang Island on 17 December 1946. The height is 762 m (2,500 ft) and the mainland can just be discerned in the background.

British War Department numbers, a Japanese C58 2-6-2 and an ex-Javanese C30 2-6-2T, as well as the resident FMSR Class I 0-6-2T No. 173 built by Kitson of Leeds in 1913.

To the left were the sidings serving the large dock area. Then the train ran through a mixture of settlements and open country, now swallowed up by concrete and steel. Soon the train reached the famous causeway, 1,080 m (3,543 ft) long. To the right could be seen various naval vessels anchored at the large base.

At Johore Bahru, seat of the Sultan of Johore, the scene changes dramatically. Some authors have implied that, because the railway builders chose to keep the ruling gradient at 1:100 and followed contours and natural routes to avoid the mountains in the interior, there was little difficulty in construction – but this is not so. As the land is situated near the equator and is subject to torrential rains, numerous watercourses cut across the line of the railway. Because of the swamps and tropical rain forest, there were few established land routes to follow. The railway had come before track and road, as most trade went by sea and river.

Consequently, the line twists and turns, crossing numerous steel bridges and at times affording tantalizing glimpses of settlements or sudden distant views. In places, great rock walls rise alongside the line and, whether riding in the coach or taking advantage of the restaurant/buffet car, an alert traveller will find much of interest throughout the journey.

Johore Bahru had a number of sidings and a locomotive stabling point. Today it is a frontier station with the usual

INFORMATION BOX

Termini	Singapore and Penang
Country	Malaya
Distance	783 km (487 miles)
Date of travel	1946

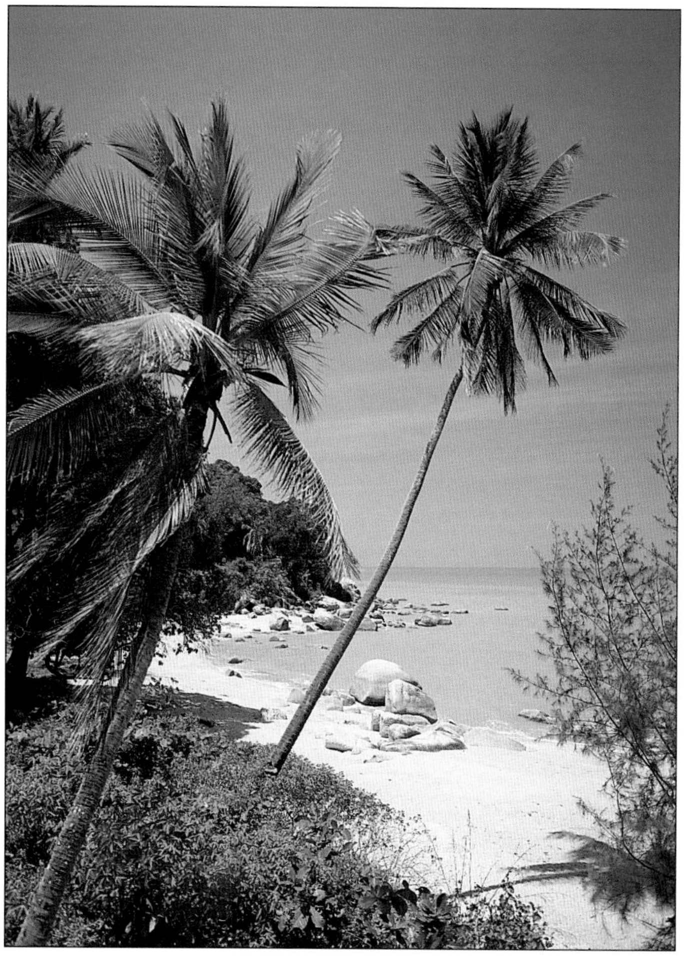

● RIGHT
On arrival at Penang, what better way to relax than a visit to the beach?

disruption to be expected at such places. Heading north, the line was fairly level and straight, passing through jungle alive with wildlife. The jungle had been cut back from the track by 50 m (164 ft) or more, as a security measure, but this was also useful in that it helped to keep natural debris off the line and improved the driver's line of vision. Where the jungle had been cleared, there was mile upon mile of rubber and palm tree plantations interspersed with villages. At Layang-Layang was a particularly extensive plantation with its own narrow-gauge railway system and exchange sidings with the FMSR.

Kluang, 113 km (70 miles) from Singapore, was a place of some importance to the railway and a passing-point. Here, two rail-mounted Jeeps (the famous, little, wartime, rough-country vehicles) lurked in the small, wooden, locomotive depot.

Gemas, 220 km (137 miles) from Singapore, was and is, the junction for the line that cuts across the country for 516 km (321 miles) to Kota Bharu on the east coast. In 1946, Gemas had two 296 m (971 ft) platforms, extensive sidings, a four-road locomotive depot with an 18.2 m (60 ft) turntable and a two-road carriage shed. Movement was controlled by two signal-boxes each with 60 levers, now replaced by a modern 80-lever frame. It was normal for locomotive crews to be changed here.

There is a short climb out of Gemas, and it is just 53 km (33 miles) to Tampin along the main line, which kept as closely as possible to the western side of the peninsula to avoid the central mountain range that rises in places to over 2,133 m (7,000 ft). Tampin was the junction for the 38 km (24 mile) branch to Malacca on the west coast, which was not re-laid after the war.

The next stretch was notable for tin mines and rubber plantations as well as paddy fields, a feature often to be found in areas cleared of jungle. At Seremban, some 61 km (38 miles) further north, was the junction for Port Dickson, which sees only freight traffic now.

In the 59 km (37 miles), to Kuala Lumpur, the whole nature of the scene changed. There were more signs of habitation, and the scars of tin mining became more evident, especially near Sungei Besi, which claimed to have the largest tin mine in the world.

At Salak South Junction a 30-lever signal-box controlled the entrance to the short Sultan Street and Ampang branches, the latter now used for oil traffic. Port Swettenham Junction, 4.8 km

● LEFT
Class L 4-6-2 No. 214 was one of the many locomotives on the dump at the severely damaged Sentul works near Kuala Lumpur in early 1946.

(3 miles) further north, had a 40-lever signal-box covering the entrance to the 43 km (27 mile) long branch to the west coast harbour of Port Swettenham and the Brickfields branch, leading to Kuala Lumpur's large freight yards.

Kuala Lumpur's ornate main passenger station still exists, with four platform faces covered by an overall roof. In 1945, it housed the headquarters of the FMSR, which now occupies a nearby office block. The two 80-lever signal-boxes have been replaced by a single 80-lever modern box.

Some 900 metres (2,953 ft) to the south of the station on the west side was situated the 28-stall roundhouse with its 18.2 m (60 ft) turntable, pre-heating water plant, mechanical coaler, ash-plant and a workshop. Three large carriage sheds served by 13 tracks were adjacent to the roundhouse, together with a carriage-washing plant. Both these depots were severely damaged in attacks by the US airforce, and in 1946 the ash-plant and coaler were not functioning and the pre-heating plant was wrecked.

Sentul locomotive, carriage and wagon works was situated about a mile down the Batu Caves branch, which diverged

● **ABOVE LEFT**
A view of Singapore's Chinatown.

● **ABOVE RIGHT**
A Swiss-built funicular railway to Summit Road on Penang Island.

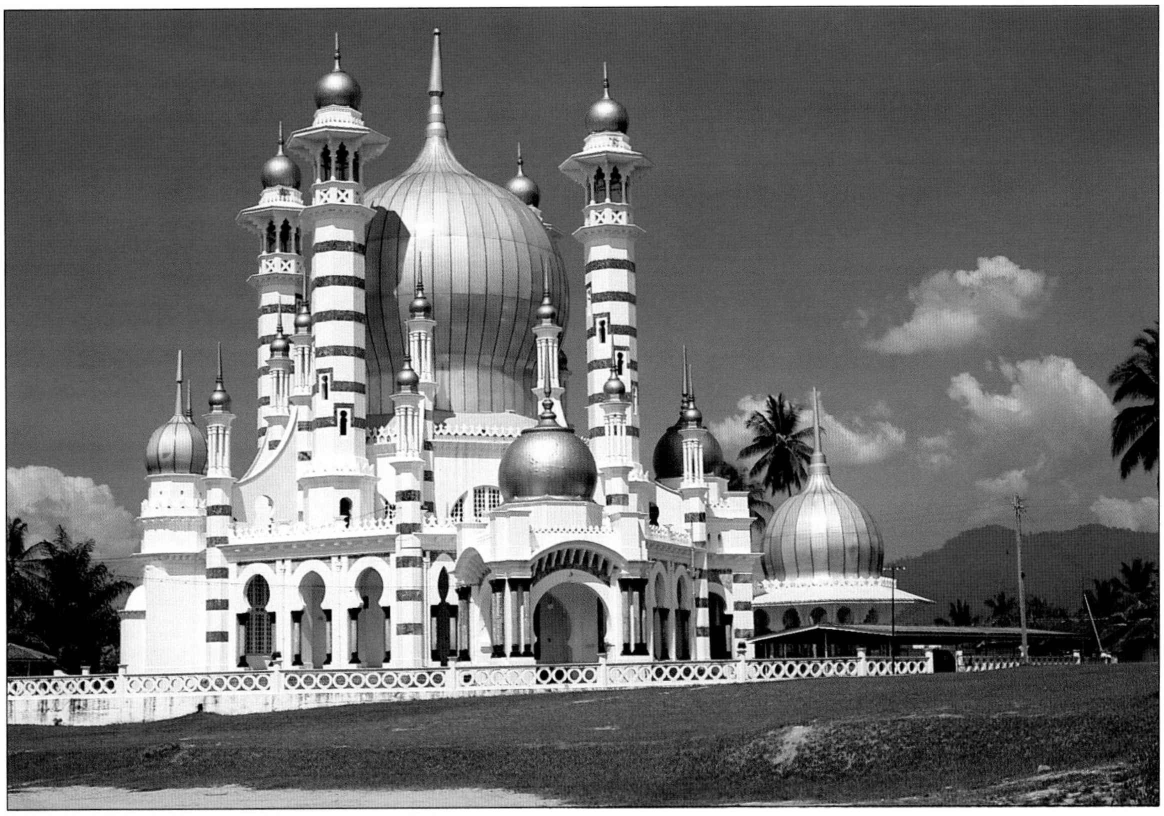

● **RIGHT**
The traveller will see many mosques from the train. One such is the Ubundian Mosque at Kuala Kangsar.

● **BELOW**
The craft in the foreground was one of the means of getting from the Malayan mainland to Penang Island. The ship in the background was a "prize of war" and renamed *Empire Rani*, 17 April 1947.

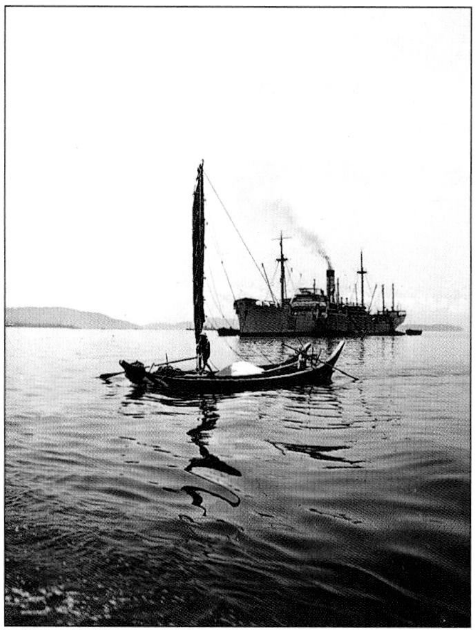

● **BELOW**
Seen in December 1946, No. 402.03, one of the powerful 4-6-4Ts of the FMSR, was used as a "banker" for trains travelling over the Taiping pass.

● **BOTTOM**
Famous throughout the world for its rubber, this is one of the many Malayan rubber plantations which will be seen from the train.

north-west about 1.6 km (1 mile) from Kuala Lumpur station. The works was divided into two sections by a 61 tonne (60 ton) electrically powered traverser. The section to the south was devoted to locomotive repairs, with iron and brass foundries, pattern shop, tin- and copper-smiths' shops, stores and an electrical sub-station. To the north were the C & W shops, electrical and train lighting repair shops, paint shop, saw mill, smithy and boiler shops.

A short distance north of Kuala Lumpur lies Kuang, the junction for a 23 km (14 mile) long branch to Batang Berjuntai on which, at the half-way point, was situated the coal mine at Batu Arang, which provided steam coal for the FMSR. From here to Tanjong Malim, the 61 km (38 miles) of line ran through open countryside but a depressing sight was the wastelands created by abandoned tin workings.

For the 124 km (77 miles) from Tanjong Malim to the important town of Ipoh, the line runs along the eastern edge of the wide coastal plain and below the foothills of the mountains. The 71 km (44 mile) section to Tapah Road, the junction for the 29 km (18 mile) branch to Telok Anson, a port on the Perak River, is largely through jungle. Tapah Road was also one of the nearest points of access to the mountain resorts in the cool and highly scenic Cameron Highlands to the west of the line.

A 24 km (15 mile) long branch heads off westward to Tromoh. At Falim, approximately 1.6 km (1 mile) down, lies the locomotive depot for Ipoh, a substantial six-road building with a workshop and an 18.2 m (60 ft) turntable. The two-storey station building was imposing, and the station boasted no fewer than five platforms.

For the author, the line from Ipoh to Prai provided the widest variety of scenery on the whole journey, for it includes the climb to the summit of the line through what was generally known as the Taiping pass. From Kuala Kangsa, the railway ascended gently through rubber plantations, but at Padang Rengas the serious climbing began. For all trains of more than 152 tonnes (150 tons), banking locomotives were provided,

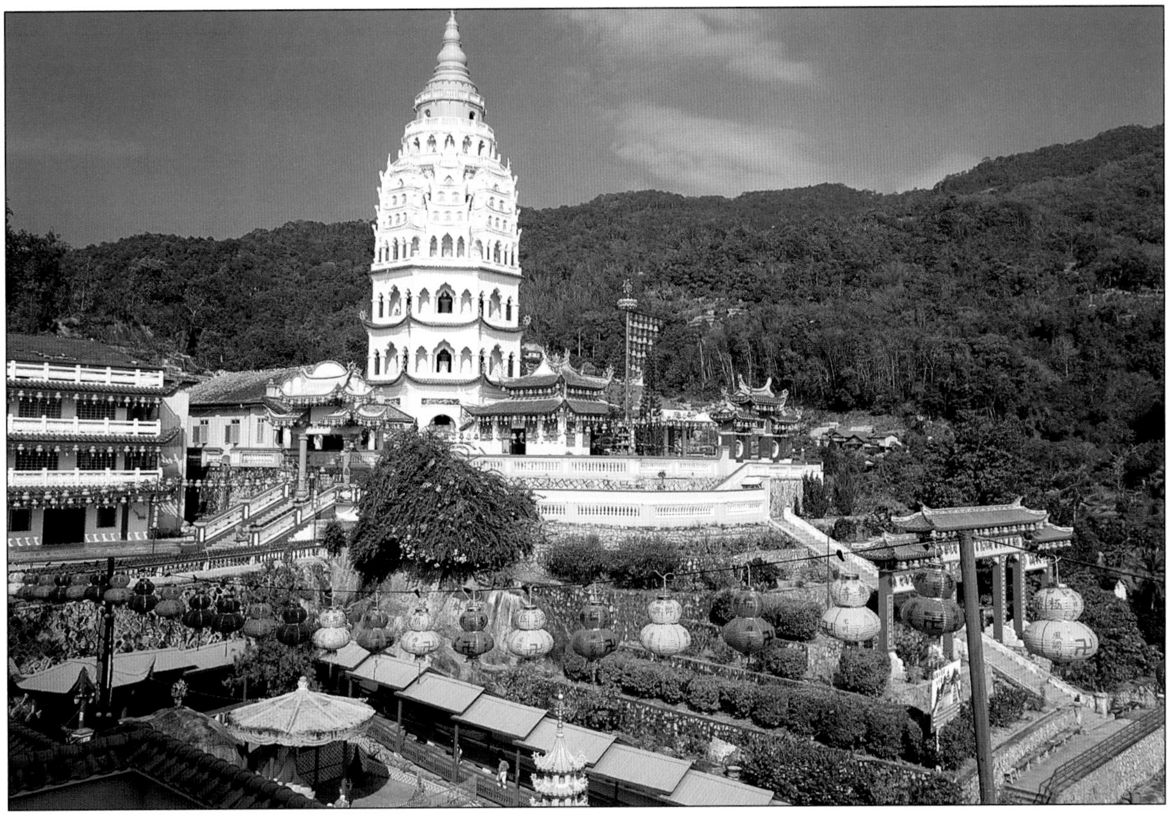

● RIGHT
Penang's Kek Lok Si Temple.

● BELOW RIGHT
A pair of the Singapore Harbour Board 0-4-0STS at Singapore shed in December 1945. No. 5, on the right, is believed to have been built by Robert Stephenson (Works No. 3346/1907).

usually Class C^2 4-6-4T from Taiping locomotive depot. For 1.6 km (1 mile) the grade is 1:80, and the scenery became spectacular as the train twisted and turned, passing now and again through tunnels, the longest of which was 345 m (1,132 ft). Emerging from one of these tunnels, the line crossed a viaduct providing a splendid view of Gunong Bondok and the valley of the Perak River. The line descended for 8.5 km (5¼ miles) from the summit at Bukit Gantang at the same 1:80 gradient, including in this section the sharpest main-line curve of 12 chains (241 m or 792 ft) radius. The maximum banked load over the pass was 660 tonnes (650 tons) if the train engine was a Class S 4-6-2, which had not only the maximum tractive effort of 13,370 kg (29,477 lbs) but also the heaviest axle load of 16.25 tonnes (16 tons). The O Class were allowed 559 tonnes (550 tons).

Taiping, in the middle of the Larut plain, was the centre for the local rubber plantations and the once extensive tin mining industry first established there some 100 years ago. It was the junction for the 12 km (7½ mile) long Port Weld branch and there were a number of sidings. Passengers were served by a sizeable station with three platform faces. Not far north of Taiping, the line passes through low hills, and then there is an 8 km (5 mile) long stretch of straight track.

The 69 km (43 miles) from Taiping to Bukit Mertajam is mostly level, and much of the terrain is marshy. From Bukit Mertajam, 775 km (481 miles) from Singapore, the line to the Siamese frontier at Padang Besar heads north, but my train took the short westward branch to Prai. This was double track, but made single by the Japanese. From Prai, I hired a native craft to take me across to Butterworth, from where the FMSR ferry was then running to the main town on Penang Island, Georgetown.

Tanahabang to Rangkasbitung

The account of this journey has been compiled from notes taken in August 1974. The journey is still possible today and is highly recommended.

Since the coaches were already packed with people, I decided to travel on the engine. There were 75 people already mounted on that locomotive – a modest 3 ft 6 in gauge secondary line diesel – of whom 23 were in the cab and the remainder on the front, sides and top. Undaunted I was hauled aboard.

Upon leaving the station, the train gingerly threaded its way through a maze of dwellings – colonization of the sidings and the disused rolling stock being considerable. One metre (3¼ ft) from the lines lay tightly packed dwellings, a mixture of tile, thatch and wood. We passed close to line-side stalls which, but for 7.6 cm (3 in), would have been collapsed by the engine.

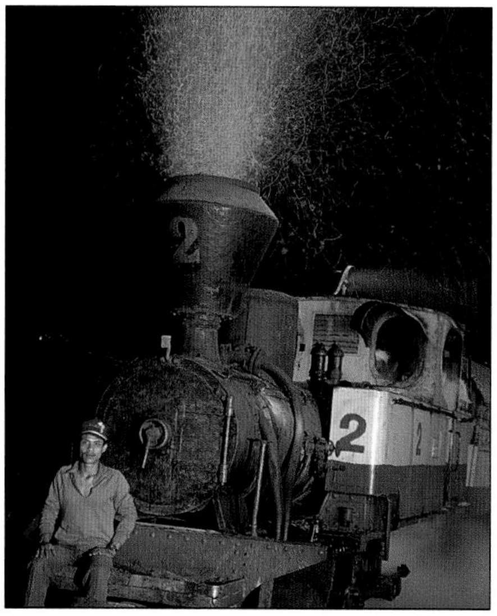

● LEFT
This scene at Kediri shows the "sandman", whose job it is to sit on the front of the locomotive and spray the tracks with sand to prevent slipping during the frequent tropical storms.

INFORMATION BOX

Termini	Tanahabang and Rangkasbitung
Country	Indonesia
Distance	*c.* 70 km (43 miles)
Date of travel	August 1974

But this colourful scene, which stretched over a considerable distance, was tinged on this occasion with another pleasure, for the simple, delightful Indonesian state flag – the upper half red, the lower white – fluttered gaily and riotously from every building, wagon and stall. It was 18 August – Independence Day. During the week of celebrations even the locomotives bear flags, attached to special mounts incorporated on to the smokebox tops.

The journey was excruciatingly bad. The diesel crawled indolently along and stops were frequent. We had scarcely covered 16 km (10 miles) before even the locals were beginning to look drowsy. The driver was wedged up in a far corner of the cab from which he could see a little of the track ahead – presumably some agreement existed with the horde on the buffer beams that, should an

● LEFT
A typical sugar plantation scene on Java, showing the temporary track beds, which bring the wagons of loaded cane to the main-line railway. The locomotive, which patiently waits in the background, was built in Leeds, England.

● RIGHT
Indonesian Independence Day celebrations on 18 August 1974, and the state flag flutters gaily on the smoke-box top of Class B51 No. 39, a two-cylinder 4-4-0 built by Werkspoor of Amsterdam. This scene at the locomotive shed at Rangkasbitung features a C27 4-6-4T in the background, an engine also built by Werkspoor and dating back to 1919.

● BELOW
A typical Javan sugar plantation worker suitably attired for protection from the razor-sharp leaves and stems of the sugar cane.

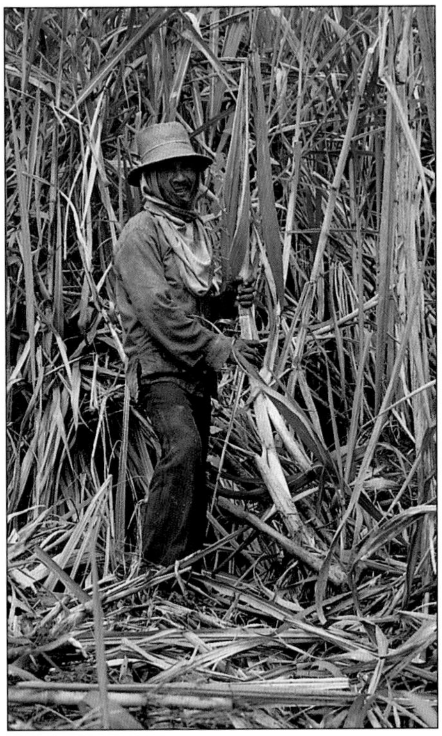

emergency arise, they must bang on the engine's sides. Such conditions underline part of the malaise of the Perusahaan Negara Kereta Api (Indonesian State Railways), in that the only passengers who ever pay on a PNKA line are those unfortunate individuals who dutifully remain in the compartment or are unable to escape the ticket-collector either by climbing out on to the coach roof or by obtaining another, equally precarious place on the train by any of 20 or more hazardous methods.

The engine, of course, is the driver's preserve; few ticket-collectors ever infiltrate that domain. My compassion for the driver on this trip was put sharply into perspective when the hat came round. This was the driver's collection – half the price of the normal fare, no tickets issued and no questions asked. Had I really thought the engine crew would suffer such discomfort for nothing? Honour among thieves was never better epitomized than by the way in which the hat finally did the round of the engine compartment and was dutifully returned to the driver full of the passengers' rupiahs.

A plume of rich brown smoke erupted from the loop ahead. We were crossing with an eastbound steam train. Despite the barrage of flags, I detected the familiar outline of a Class 27 4-6-4T, built by Armstrong Whitworth of Newcastle upon Tyne in 1922, hauling an unbelievably well patronized six-coach Independence Day Special. Nearly five hours after leaving Tanahabang, the journey over the Javan paddy fields was over as the train crawled into the small town of Rangkasbitung.

● LEFT
A Class C12 06, seen against one of Java's famous sunsets, following the Independence Day celebrations.

Rangkasbitung to Labuan

The unintended journey started with my inspection of a Werkspoor engine of 1909, a B51, which was standing idle in a siding at Rangkasbitung. Utterly fascinated, I entered the vacant cab. However, the Javan crew soon arrived and with an incomprehensible acknowledgement of my presence proceeded to back down on to a rake of decrepit rolling stock lying in the station. Suddenly the engine moved forward, and the unexpected journey began.

I had no idea where I was going and, although the crew were friendly enough, the language barrier made communication impossible. The epic way in which B5138 stormed out of Rangkasbitung that evening did justice to her Prussian lineage as, with trilling whistle, she charged through the suburbs and out of town.

Although the B51 burned a mixture of coal, wood and oil, during the journey's early stages the fireman was principally using coal. Dusk was rapidly advancing and soon our engine was pumping black exhaust into an azure sky, a pungently smelling frothy smoke, which continually swept round the cab and down the train. Our speed was greater than I had thought possible as the engine ferociously headed through the darkening landscape. The veteran's violent lurching over the rough track beds was stimulating enough, though on the few occasions when she was eased a pleasant aroma of coal smoke wafted back through the fire-hole door and into the cab.

• BELOW
The constant flurry of sparks that emanate from the chimneys of Java's steam locomotives is epitomized in this scene of a Class B50 2-4-0 built by Sharp Stewart of Manchester in 1885.

• BOTTOM
A typically decrepit Javan passenger-train, consisting of wooden-bodied four-wheeled coaches and hauled by B50 2-4-0 No. 14.

INFORMATION BOX

Termini	Rangkasbitung and Labuan
Country	Indonesia
Distance	*c.* 55 km (34 miles)
Date of travel	August 1974

Darkness had fallen by the time we reached the first station – a wayside halt, which only merited our presence for a matter of seconds.

Soon the drama returned in all its affray. A hiss of steam escaping from the front end became audible and made an exciting foil to the throbbing rasps of exhaust. Speed mounted terrifyingly, and the engine became a mass of churning, pulsating machinery. The whistle screamed and wailed in long eerie bursts as we sped past lonely villages and small ungated crossings, but remote as we were and dark as it was, a few ox carts could invariably be discerned momentarily lit up by the swirling incandescence of B5138's fire.

Without warning she hit a downgrade, and the engine was really opened out. The roar became hypnotic. It was impossible to estimate our speed, the darkness outside revealing nothing from which a bearing might be taken. The crew, bathed in a shimmering orange glow, clung tenaciously to the cab sides. The fire, white hot, lit up the black exhaust trail, which raced in a swirling slipstream above the cab roof. It certainly felt as if we could to all intents and purposes have been hitting one hundred miles per hour (160 kph)!

I had come to Indonesia to find a locomotive dinosaur and by perfect fortune had found one in triumphant full cry – the last of her breed, a Prussian phantom and a living ghost of the great 19th-century steam age. With many kilometres now behind us it seemed that the country was beginning to flatten out and fireflies could be seen over the rice fields. It was about this time that our coal supply ran out, and the logs that had hitherto been ignored came into their own. The B51 responded in a flurry of sparks, brilliantly cascading in the paths of the fireflies. Suddenly, as the train sped onwards through different terrain, the fireflies were left behind, and, like the eclipse of a fireworks display observed with the awe of childhood, the magic was gone.

Soon we slowed down and speckled lights could be seen ahead. We had reached our destination.

• ABOVE
An Indonesian State Railways Class B51 4-4-0 takes water at Rangkasbitung. The Prussian ancestry of this German-built veteran of 1902 is in full evidence.

• LEFT
A brace of Class B51 4-4-0s – including No. 38 on which the footplate journey took place – raise steam in the depot yard at Labuan.

PORT AUGUSTA TO ALICE SPRINGS
THE GHAN

The heart of Australia has seen little potential for development beyond minerals and cattle stations. To serve the few hardy settlers who ventured into this harsh country in the early days, Afghans brought in the supplies with their camel teams. As the need for transport grew, the South Australian government commenced the construction of a narrow-gauge railway from Port Augusta in South Australia, first to serve the anticipated wheat and wool traffic in the false belief that "rain would follow the plough", and then to tap the minerals and cattle from further north.

The line to Hergott Springs, now Marree, was opened for traffic in 1884. This was the end of the famous Birdsville Track and a meeting-point for several cattle-driving routes. Three mixed trains a week handled the traffic. Beyond there, the line was constructed as Unemployment Relief and in 1891 reached Oodnadatta, 769 km (478 miles) from Port Augusta. At first, one mixed train a week handled this extension, but this was soon reduced to one a fortnight, with trains averaging 19 kph (12 mph). In 1911 the Commonwealth Government became owners of the line, but did not take control of operations until 1916. They continued building the line, supposed to continue on to Darwin on the northern coast, stopping construction at Alice Springs, 471 km (293 miles) further north. The mixed

● LEFT
Following World War II, the Commonwealth Railways imported luxurious air-conditioned cars from Wegmann in Germany for the transcontinental service between Port Augusta and Kalgoorlie. These included a rounded observation car, seen here at Port Augusta in 1964.

INFORMATION BOX

THE GHAN

Termini	Port Augusta and Alice Springs
Country	Australia
Distance	1,240 km (770 miles)
Date of opening	1891

● LEFT
Early settlers believed that rain would follow the plough and called this place Farina, hoping it would become the heart of the wheat belt of South Australia. But rain did not follow, and the fields had to be abandoned. Little remained when this enthusiast special Ghan travelled the standard gauge of the 1964 period. Today, even the rails are gone as a new standard-gauge route further west bypasses this area.

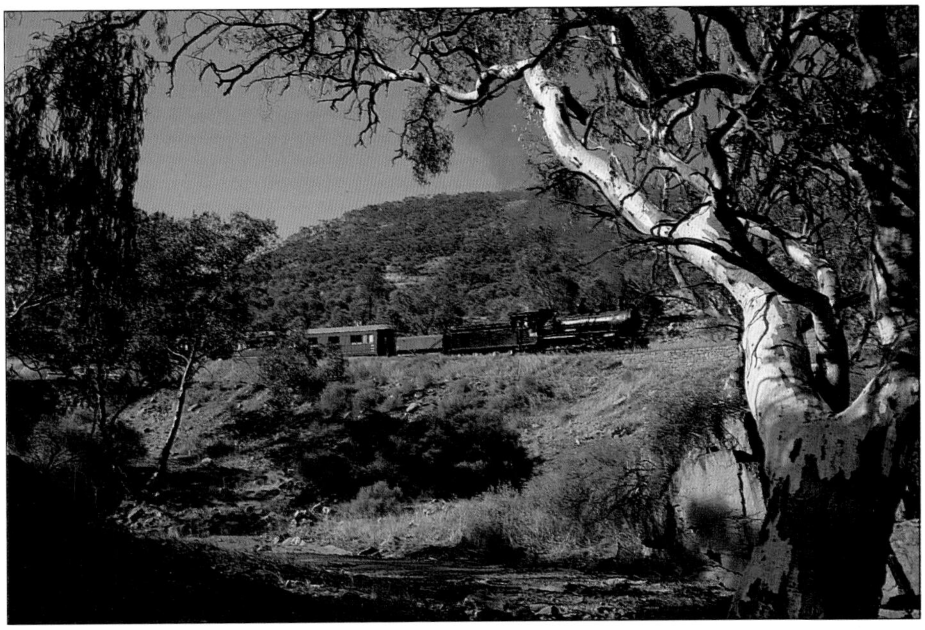

● **RIGHT**
An NM Class steam locomotive of the Commonwealth Railways, with a water gin, heads a tour train through the scenic Pichi Richi pass.

train that served this line became known as "The Ghan" in honour of the previous traders. This ran twice a week, while another service known as the "slow" travelled weekly.

Travelling on the Ghan was truly an adventure. The first section of the line through the Pichi Richi Pass was very scenic; its magnificent river gum trees are a notable feature of an area currently exploited by rail enthusiasts running the Pichi Richi Railway. The line continued alongside and through the Flinders Ranges, made famous by many painters in Australia, and then through flat salt bush country and on to Marree. Between there and Alice Springs, the lightly ballastered track was subject to sand drifts and on occasions to sudden downpours that caused washaways, making the route impassable until repairs could be effected. Passengers starting out on what was supposed to be a three-day journey could suddenly find themselves marooned in the desert for up to several weeks, with food drops from aircraft not being uncommon.

As the narrow-gauge route through the Pichi Richi pass and the Flinders Ranges limited the loads hauled, a new standard-gauge line was constructed to join the old route near Brachina, beyond which the line was standardized to Marree. In view of the problems with the line beyond Marree, it was decided in the 1970s to build a complete new standard-gauge line from near Port Augusta on a more direct route to Alice Springs bypassing virtually all of the old route, leaving everywhere beyond the Leigh Creek coalfields to more or less disappear.

Today, with standard gauge reaching Adelaide's suburbs, the only adventure on this trip – weekly in summer and twice weekly in the cooler months – is the taxi journey out of town to the standard-gauge terminal, no doubt put there to discourage patronage. From there, you ride a luxury air-conditioned train in pampered comfort. The wonders of the "Red Heart" of Australia are certainly well worth seeing, but it is not recommended in summer for those not prepared for temperatures that can rise as high as 50°C (122°F).

● **ABOVE**
The real railway adventure in Australia was "The Ghan", originally all narrow gauge, running from Port Augusta in South Australia to Alice Springs in the Northern Territory. The starting-point was the exchange platform at Port Augusta.

● **ABOVE**
An early vehicle used in Government Railway days in the vicinity of the Pichi Richi pass was a Kitson steam rail motor. Coffee Pot, as it is affectionately known, has been restored and is again in periodic service for tourist groups. Here it is undergoing servicing in the Quorn workshops of the Pichi Richi Railway.

SYDNEY TO BRISBANE
THE BRISBANE EXPRESS

In the 1960s, two trains running on entirely different routes were both called the Brisbane Express. For travellers in a hurry, and with little interest in the journey itself, there was the one using the newer 1,035 km (643 mile) coastal route, much of the journey being done in darkness. This service was actually divided into two, with the Brisbane Limited Express doing the journey in 15½ hours and the slower Brisbane Express following in 17 hours and 50 minutes.

For the tourist, the older route had far more to offer, and although it did include a night section, enjoyable stretches of scenic country were traversed in daylight. By the 1965 timetable, an early afternoon departure of 13.55 meant that the descent of the Cowan Bank and the crossing of the Hawkesbury River would be done in good light, as would the run along the shores of Brisbane Waters. There was well inhabited country as far as Wyong and then timbered hilly country nearly to Broadmeadow, the junction for trains to Newcastle. This was coal mining country, and a considerable amount of coal traffic would be seen on the way to Maitland, where the shorter coastal route branched off to the north. The "Main" route continued westwards through relatively flat dairy country to Singleton, passing through there about dusk. In the darkness, the line began a gradual climb towards the foothills of the Great Dividing Range via Murrurundi, the depot town for push-up and assistant engines used by heavy traffic crossing the range from both directions. The ruling gradient there was 1:40 on both sides, and provided many a spectacle as locomotives struggled up the 8 km (5 miles) of steep bank to Ardglen tunnel.

To the west of the range, the line dropped in easier stages to Tamworth before climbing the Moonbi Range to the Northern Tablelands. Daylight came in the beautiful hilly country before Tenterfield, the last major town before the Queensland border. Less than 18 km (11 miles) brought the train to the border and the change-of-gauge station at Wallangarra. Here the narrow-gauge express to Brisbane waited to continue the journey through more scenic hilly country to some of the finest rural land

● **BELOW**
The express on the long and arduous ascent to Toowoomba. The vehicle behind the second locomotive is a water gin, which is used to augment the supply in the engines' tenders.

INFORMATION BOX

THE BRISBANE EXPRESS	
Termini	Sydney and Brisbane
Country	Australia
Distance	1,150 km (715 miles)
Date of opening	1888

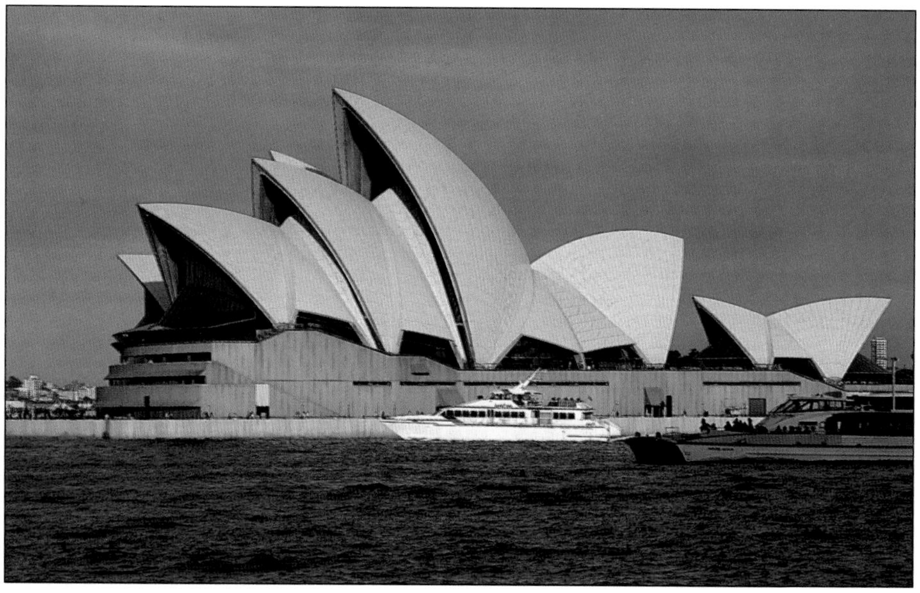

● **ABOVE**
The famous and familiar sight of Sydney Harbour Bridge.

● **OPPOSITE BOTTOM**
One of the world's best-known landmarks is Sydney Opera House.

● **BELOW LEFT**
The view from Sydney centre looking down William Street to King's Cross.

● **BELOW RIGHT**
Part of the climb facing the early Brisbane-Sydney expresses near Toowoomba in Queensland. The diesel-hauled goods train is carefully easing itself down the first part of the descent towards Brisbane, Toowoomba being just over the crest in the middle background.

in Australia, the Darling Downs. After 5½ hours, the train reached the beautiful city of Toowoomba, famous for the magnificent gardens created by the local inhabitants.

The descent of the mountains from Toowoomba was an immensely scenic but very time-consuming journey. Because of this, the Queensland Railways had a co-ordinated bus/rail service between Toowoomba and Helidon at the bottom of the range, and Brisbane-bound travellers could spend over an hour in Toowoomba, eating, sightseeing or whatever. They could then catch the bus and rejoin the train at Heildon for the final run into Brisbane. This option, however, meant that they missed much of the beauty of that part of the journey. In the reverse direction, Toowoomba dwellers could get home an hour ahead of the train by using the bus. The arrival in Brisbane would be shortly after dusk at 18.26 – 28½ hours after leaving Sydney, a run of 1,150 km (715 miles). Today this journey is no more, as a considerable length of the line from Glen Innes to the Queensland border has been abandoned.

BROKEN HILL TO ADELAIDE
THE BROKEN HILL EXPRESS

For centuries, man has dreamed of the pot of gold at the end of the rainbow, and prospectors have trudged into the wilderness in search of their fortune.

Few areas could have been more dismal than the country near the South Australian-New South Wales border. However, as early as 1876, galena (lead sulphide) was found on the NSW side, and by 1883 the Silverton area was booming with mines and even smelters. In the same year, galena was discovered at Broken Hill. The South Australian Government, seeing the potential of the area, hastily built a narrow-gauge line from Peterborough (then Petersburg) to the border, reaching there in January 1887, but it was not permitted to cross the border by the NSW government. This led to the formation of the private Silverton Tramway Company, later known as Broken Hill's gold mine. By this time Silverton, a town with 36 hotels, was declining rapidly. However, Broken Hill, though now declining, has been a boom town for all this century.

Though in NSW, Broken Hill is included in the South Australian time zone, and most commercial business is conducted with the closer capital city of Adelaide. To make this connection a regular train service connected the two cities, with the Broken Hill Express being one of the few passenger expresses in Australia hauled for many years by Garratt locomotives. The others were in Queensland. This was basically an overnight service, and the South Australian Railway (SAR) built up the tonnage with freight wagons, thereby making it a mixed train.

To the east of the border, the Silverton Tramway Company, with its 58 km (36 miles) of line, provided the locomotives and a percentage of the freight wagons. The original locomotives were Colonial Moguls, followed in 1912 by the A Class, very English-looking 4-6-0s. In 1951, the W Class 4-8-2 semi-streamlined locomotives, similar to those used in Western Australia, took over before being replaced by 673kW Co-Co diesel electrics from 1960 to 1970, when the standard gauge bypassed the private line.

Early traffic on the South Australian side was handled by Y or X Class Moguls, but with the growing traffic bigger locomotives were soon needed, with the Chief Mechanical Engineer designing the highly successful T Class 4-8-0s, 78 of which were built from 1903 onwards, with some remaining in service right to

• ABOVE
Between Terowie and Adelaide, the broad-gauge Broken Hill Express could have been handled by a variety of locomotives, the most eye-catching being the streamlined 520 Class. For a short period, the 23 km (14 miles) between Terowie and the main junction town of Peterborough had a third rail added to eliminate a short journey on narrow gauge where the standard gauge reached Peterborough. Here No. 526 works a broad-gauge route to Adelaide, that spelt the end of this section, leaving the once important break-of-gauge town of Terowie to become a ghost town.

• BELOW
The Broken Hill Express travelled most of its journey in darkness. Enthusiasts wishing to re-create the journey in daylight arranged for South Australian Railway's Garratt No. 402 to haul the train, seen here passing the isolated Mannahill station heading north.

INFORMATION BOX

The Broken Hill Express	
Termini	Broken Hill and Adelaide
Country	Australia
Distance	582 km (362 miles)
Date of opening	1887

● **ABOVE**
The Broken Hill Express was worked by the Silverton Tramway Company on the New South Wales side of the border and a South Australian Garratt on their side of the fence. Here we see a re-enactement of the border change.

the end of the steam era. These brought the train 225 km (140 miles) to Terowie, where one changed to the broad gauge, with an S Class 4-4-0 continuing the 225 km (140 mile) journey to Adelaide until the arrival of larger engines of the Webb era in the mid-1920s.

In 1953, the 400 Class Garratts arrived and rapidly took over the Broken Hill traffic. From 1959, the SAR began acquiring 830 Class Co-Co diesel electrics, which eventually replaced steam on this semi-desert route. This standardization rang the death knell for the Broken Hill Express with the Indian Pacific eventually taking over the passenger traffic on the line and the broad-gauge services being withdrawn from Terowie.

According to a 1953 timetable, the Broken Hill Express would depart from Broken Hill at 19.48 behind a Silverton W Class, covering what was possibly the most scenic part of this semi-desert journey in darkness to the border, arriving at 21.21. Here a 400 Class Garratt took over for the run to Peterborough, where passengers for Port Pirie had to make an 03.58 change of train. From there the train reversed, with a new locomotive for the short run to Terowie, where Adelaide passengers changed to the broad gauge at 04.50. After a 20-minute allowance for refreshments, the broad-gauge train headed for an 09.20 arrival in Adelaide.

● **ABOVE RIGHT**
The Adelaide skyline.

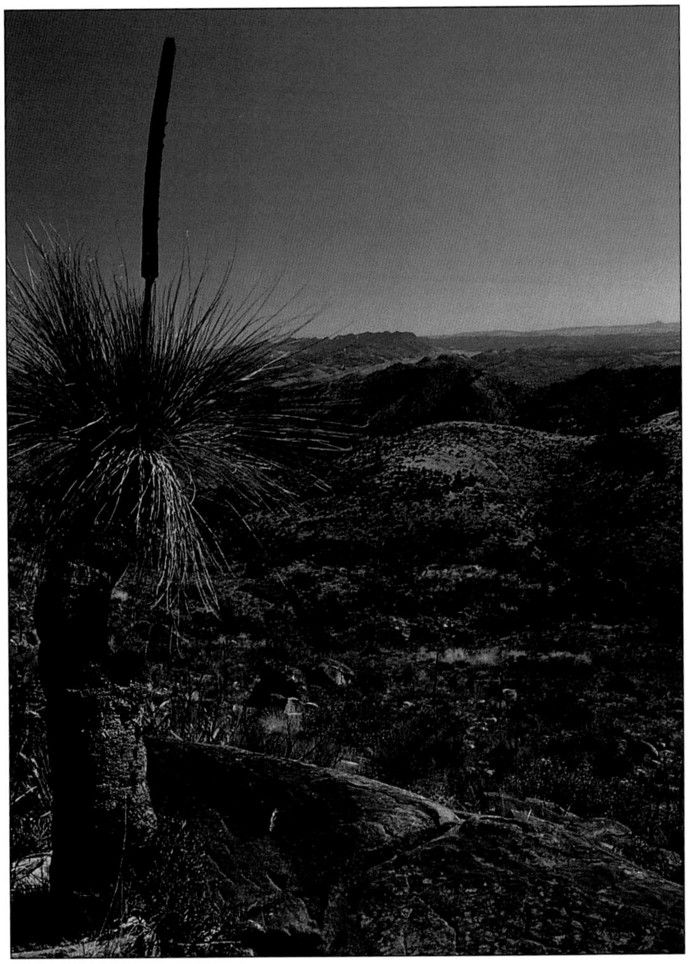

● **RIGHT**
This plant, called Black Boy, is common along the route of the Broken Hill Express.

Brisbane to Cairns The Sunshine Rail Experience

Probably more than the other Australian states, Queensland relied on coastal shipping to service the large number of ports on its long coastline. This resulted in railways being built, but not along the coast. They were built as isolated lines running inland from the various ports. As passengers began demanding quicker and more reliable services from Brisbane to the northern centres, the Government began constructing lines to connect the various isolated sections. It was, however, not until the end of 1924 that it was possible to travel all the way, 1,679 km (1,043 miles), to Cairns in the far north.

The lines were lightly built with low-level bridges not far above the river beds. To the Government's surprise, the railways gained a considerable amount of goods traffic, and rural industry, particularly sugar, expanded rapidly. In the beginning, a trip to the north took 52 hours, which included a 24-hour stay in Townsville along the way. Services were soon improved, with the 1950 Sunshine Express departing Brisbane at 20.00 and arriving at Cairns two days later at 16.00.

However, time brought great changes. First came dieselization, and then the gaining of massive coal contracts by mines inland from the coastal ports. Lines had to be upgraded and realigned in many areas, new bridges built and Centralized Traffic Control introduced. Steam trains could handle a reasonable depth of floodwater when there was no

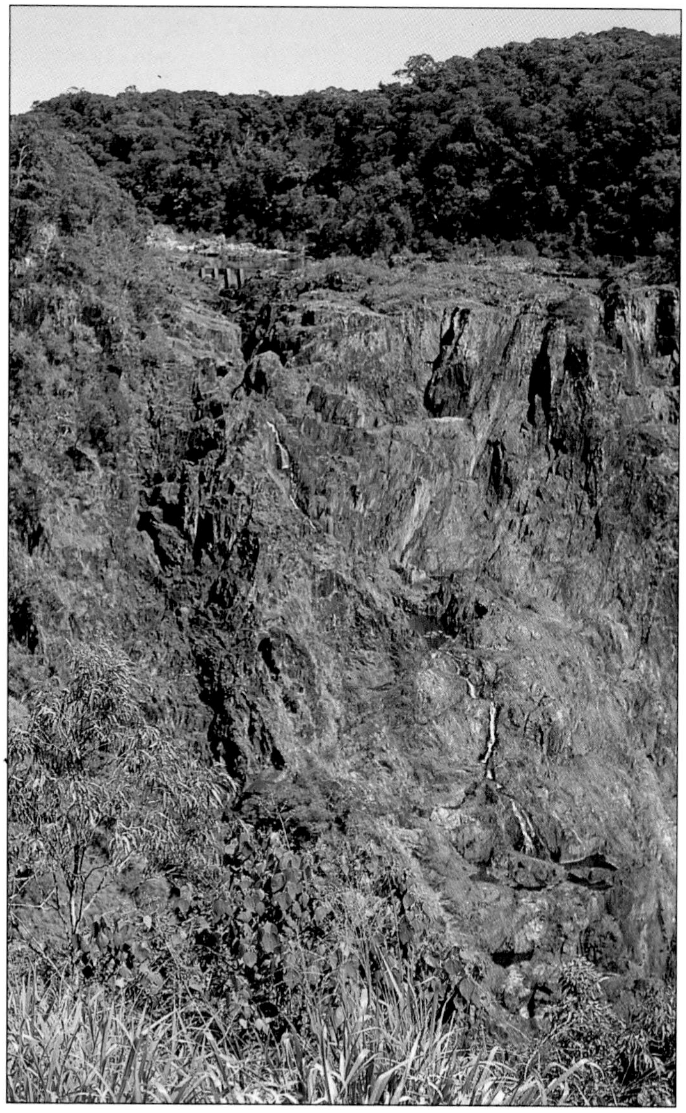

● ABOVE
One of the attractions of Kuranda is the waterfalls.

● ABOVE
No trip to Cairns in the far north of Queensland is complete without the final excursion to Kuranda, battling up the cliff faces with magnificent views of the coast, cane fields, rain forest, waterfalls and finally the enchanting market village of Kuranda.

● ABOVE
When steam was king in Queensland, the expresses between Brisbane and Cairns would have been worked by these beautiful BB18 1/4 Class Pacifics with their comfortable wooden coaches. A tour train stands at Nambour, typifying an express of the period. Parochial rail fans from interstate would often sing "I'll Walk Beside You" whenever Queensland trains were mentioned – hardly fair, as they provided a very efficient and reasonably speedy service in steam days and are now probably the most modern in the country.

● LEFT
The dieselized air-conditioned Sunlander express rumbles through the cane fields near Feluga in North Queensland in 1971.

appreciable current. With one leading, and another locomotive at the rear to steady the train, they could run down into a river and work their way across. This was completely out of the question for a diesel electric, so new high-level bridges were a must.

In the late 1950s, Queensland's magnificent Garratts brought 406 tonnes (400 tons) of coal to the coast. In the 1980s, six diesel electric locomotives, three leading and three in the middle of the train with Locotrol radio control, were bringing in over 10,000 tonnes (10,160 tons) at a time.

Electrification was the answer for this heavy traffic, and coal lines were electrified together with the coastal line from Brisbane to Rockhampton in 1989. Now luxury express trains such as the Queenslander cover the distance to Cairns in only 32 hours and 5 minutes.

With the connection of the isolated systems, to build maintenance depots for the new locomotives and railcars all over the State would have been a costly exercise, so most major work was carried out near Brisbane. Some person capable of lateral thinking, realizing that returning rail motors from the branch lines for periodic overhaul over this great distance was a slow and costly exercise, came up with the idea of using the trips to carry tourists, with local sightseeing trips laid on as a feature during the driver's rest periods.

While the expresses race over the distance in less than one-and-a-half days three times a week, the rail motor exchange has developed into an exciting weekly six-day train tour, now with a loco-hauled train. It includes accommodation in quality hotels overnight and numerous trips to points of special interest, such as a boat tour to the Barrier Reef.

Unlike most lengthy rail journeys in Australia, there is no let up to the magnificent scenery for the full length of the railway line, be it Mother Nature or the rural properties, which are seen at their best in early spring. For the rail fan, too, there is the heavy traffic to be seen *en route*, and during the cane season, from August to November, a multitude of 2 ft gauge trains are busy rushing cane to the mills and sugar to the ports. Indeed, the highlights of the journey are not over on reaching Cairns. Further exciting rail trips can be started from there, such as the magnificent climb to Kuranda, rising along the cliff face past waterfalls, or, with the help of buses, tours can reach the Mount Surprise line and the famous Croydon-Normanton line.

INFORMATION BOX

Termini	Brisbane and Cairns
Country	Australia
Distance	1,679 km (1,043 miles)
Date of opening	1924

● RIGHT
The train from Cairns approaches Kuranda.

PORT KEMBLA TO MOSS VALE THE COCKATOO RUN

In a deal involving the establishment of a steelworks at Port Kembla in New South Wales, the Government agreed to construct a railway line up the steep mountainsides to connect the new industrial area with the Main Southern Railway at Moss Vale, thus providing a shorter and cheaper link to the interstate markets in the south. The new line, approximately 70 km (43 miles) in length, was opened in 1932 and has handled heavy goods traffic, mainly coal, limestone and steel products, ever since.

• LEFT
Several short journeys can often provide more pleasure and excitement than one long journey lacking in variety. A day trip in NSW is the Cockatoo Run from Port Kembla to Moss Vale and return. A stop is made at Summit Tank for passengers to experience the magnificent view over the coastline.

Passenger-traffic has been rather light, as much of the line is through a water catchment area where the entry of people, the worst polluters, is discouraged. This passenger-traffic was usually handled by rail motors or two- and three-car passenger-trains. Many of the travellers have been tourists, as this is the most scenic line in NSW, rivalled only by the now abandoned Dorrigo branch.

The line leaves the coastal Illawarra line at Unanderra and almost immediately starts on a 1:30 gradient with magnificent views of the coast. This steep gradient is almost continuous until Summit Tank, some 20 km ($12^1/_2$ miles) up the mountainside. While the coast cannot be seen from the line at Summit Tank, time has always been allowed for tourists to walk a few steps to a lookout on the cliff edge for a view of the coast.

As this relatively short section of track became congested during World War II, with heavy steam-hauled goods trains taking over an hour in the section, it became necessary to provide a crossing loop within the section. Due to the difficult terrain, the Dombarton crossing facility was unique in NSW. Trains ascended up the mountainside and branched off to the left into a level dead-end siding on a slight rise. This rise gave the train a start for rejoining the main line, on its left, on to another dead-end

• LEFT
As the Port Kembla-Moss Vale line in NSW competed for first place as the State's most scenic line, fairly regular triple-headed tours were run over this steep line. Here in 1966 at Ocean View, approaching the summit of the line, three of the famous P or C32 Class locomotives struggle up the grade towards some enthusiastic photographers.

● LEFT
In the days of government operation of passenger services on the route of the Cockatoo Run, this traffic was usually handled by railmotors or short trains hauled by a tank-engine. Here a C-30 Class tank-engine bites into the 1:30 grade with a few light carriages, a short distance out of Port Kembla in 1967.

INFORMATION BOX

Termini	Port Kembla and Moss Vale
Country	Australia
Distance	70 km (43 miles)
Date of opening	1932

siding parallel to that used by the ascending trains. When the line was clear, the train backed into the first dead-end siding used by the ascending trains before again proceeding downhill. This parallel siding for descending trains also gave some protection to the other train in the case of a runaway. The line is also subject to rock falls, and concrete shelters similar to snowsheds have been erected in the worst sections to protect it.

Summit Tank, at 579 m (1,900 ft) above sea level, is a normal crossing loop and has a turntable for turning the third locomotive used to assist heavy goods, trains and allow it to return to the coast. From here the grade eases, with even a few downward stretches and with nothing worse than 1:60 compensated for curvature to the highest point near St Anthony's. Beyond here, it is relatively flat all the way to Moss Vale.

Dieselization improved running times and increased train loads, but it also brought problems. The slow continuous grind up the mountainside, with no activity required from the driver and the continuous rumble of the motor behind him, lulled drivers to sleep and resulted in two head-on smashes. This hastened the introduction of "vigilance controls" on locomotives, forcing drivers to react at quite short intervals, and thus keeping them alert. Today, the goods traffic continues, but passenger traffic is handled by an enthusiast group known as 3801 Limited who run trains four times a week. Steam haulage is used, except in the summer months when a diesel hydraulic locomotive substitutes.

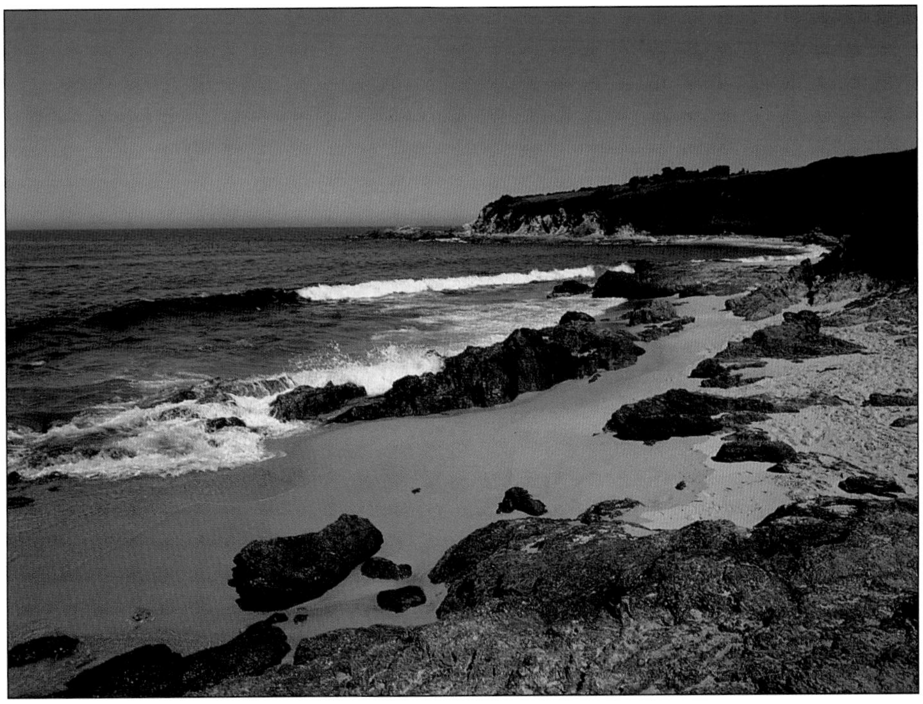

● ABOVE RIGHT
Once off the train, there are some unique road signs to be seen.

● RIGHT
This journey passes some beautiful coastal scenery.

SYDNEY TO PERTH
FROM THE PACIFIC TO THE INDIAN OCEAN

Although railway construction in Australia proceeded in earnest from the 1850s, it was not until 1917 that it was possible to cross the continent from ocean to ocean, a distance then of 4,352 km (2,704 miles) by rail. When this journey became possible, Australia was caught up in a muddle of different railway gauges, making this trip quite an adventure for travellers who were rail enthusiasts, but something of a nightmare for those who were not. The current route is standard gauge and fairly direct, but in those days it was necessary to travel via Melbourne and Adelaide.

● LEFT
A triple restoration: the Great Zigzag on the western side of the Blue Mountains in NSW, with Queensland Railway's express passenger locomotive BB18 1/4 No. 1072 hauling a set of ex-South Australian narrow-gauge cars. The popularity of this restored feat of engineering has resulted in trains running daily through this spectacular countryside for the pleasure of tourists.

According to timetables published shortly after the opening of the transcontinental line, a traveller from Sydney would board his standard gauge train at 19.25 on, say, Sunday evening and travel throughout the night to the Victorian border at Albury, where at 07.23 he had 23 minutes to change to a broad-gauge train that would arrive at Melbourne at 12.51. Here there was another change, to a broad-gauge train departing at 16.30 and again travelling overnight to arrive in Adelaide, South Australia, at 09.55 on Tuesday. Fifty minutes later, he would be on yet another broad-gauge train (no through carriages on any of these services) northwards to Terowie, where half an hour was allowed for refreshments and a change to a narrow-gauge train. This then worked its way by a circuitous route to Port Augusta,

INFORMATION BOX

Termini	Sydney and Perth
Country	Australia
Distance	3,961 km (2,461 miles) since 1970
Date of opening	1917

● LEFY
An XPT Intercity express speeds along the deviation, including ten tunnels, that was used to bypass the old zigzag at Lithgow. The viaducts and old formation now carry tourists in 3 ft 6 in gauge regular services.

arriving at 22.05 on Tuesday for the next change – this time a standard-gauge train for the journey across the Nullarbor Plains.

Over a day and a half would now be spent crossing this semi-desert, with the longest straight in the world, 478 km (297 miles), to reach the gold-mining town of Kalgoorlie at 13.38 on Thursday. Here he had a lengthier stop, no doubt for a little tourist activity, as the narrow-gauge express to Perth did not leave until 17.15, with an 09.47 arrival at Perth on Friday morning. The whole journey had taken just over four-and-a-half days, allowing for the two-hour time difference between the two sides of the continent. For the period, the trains were suitably comfortable, but these stops and changes – and the scramble for food, supplied at stations and not on the train – must have been somewhat irritating.

It was not until 1969 that the route via Broken Hill to Perth was completely standardized, and in 1970 the Indian Pacific service was inaugurated, cutting the journey down to 3,961 km (2,461 miles) and a running time of just over two-and-a-half days. Since then, a standard-gauge line has been laid almost into Adelaide and, unlike European railway systems that would provide through cars, for use from Melbourne through Adelaide to Port Pirie to attach to the train, the Indian Pacific takes a lengthy and time-consuming side jaunt from near Crystal Brook to Keswick in the Adelaide suburbs and back. This must cause frustration to through passengers.

Today, after departing from the Sydney terminal at 14.55, the train is soon through Sydney's inner suburbs and at Blacktown is on the "speedway", a fairly straight and level run on which trains are known to attain their best speeds. After crossing the Hawkesbury River beyond Penrith, the train begins the climb into the Blue Mountains. The current route is the third ascent of the mountains, the first having been a zigzag. This starts as a cut on the side of a cliff face with spectacular views. A 1:60 grade is fairly consistent as far as Valley Heights, where the real climb begins. Originally, this was continuous 1:30 with numerous 8 chain (20 m/66 ft) radius curves, but most of these curves have been improved to better than 11 chains and the grade to 1:33. Spectacular views continue to the western descent. Beautiful rolling agricultural country continues as far as Parkes, but by now the train is running in darkness. From there it is semi-desert almost all the way to Perth.

● ABOVE
Prior to the standardization of the east-west route across Australia, most travellers would have preferred the journey through Melbourne to the slow narrow-gauge journey from Broken Hill in NSW to Port Pirie in South Australia. Now, having lost this traffic, Melbourne is still a very busy railway centre, as seen in this view of the approaches to Spencer Street station.

● BELOW
As in many parts of the world, Australia has seen a decline in rail passenger traffic in recent years. Thirty years ago, many of the major expresses, especially at holiday time, had to be run in several divisions to cope with the loading. The Overland, making the connection between Melbourne and Adelaide on the east-west route, was one such train. The second division is seen here crossing the Murray River Bridge.

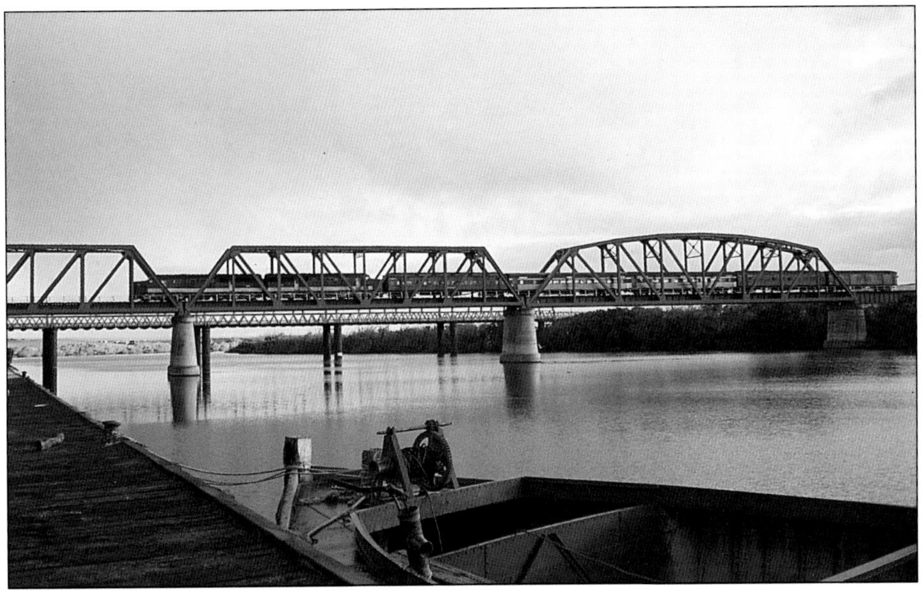

BROKEN HILL TO SULPHIDE JUNCTION

Although passenger expresses tend to dominate railway enthusiasts' records, there is one goods train that has achieved an equal fame. This was simply known as the W-44 block ore concentrate train from Broken Hill to Sulphide Junction.

Although the South Australian Railways had been reaping the revenue from silver, lead and zinc ore haulage from the rich Broken Hill mines since 1888, the New South Wales Railway did not enter competition until 1927. This was at the same time that the east coast was joined to the isolated Menindee to Broken Hill line. Sulphide Corporation had already established zinc smelters at Cockle Creek, near Newcastle, and had been taking the Broken Hill ore by train over 400 km (249 miles) to Port Pirie in South Australia. They then shipped it another 2,000 km (1,243 miles) by sea to Newcastle for further transfer to Cockle Creek. The new line made it possible to take the ore by train 1,252 km (778 miles) direct to the smelter.

The first part of this journey to be affected was the semi-desert area between Broken Hill and Parkes, where steam haulage was rapidly replaced by 49 Class Co-Co units. These 875 hp units were specially pressurized to keep out the dust on this 679 km (422 mile) first stretch over hot and dusty plains. The block train consisted of 16-bogie concentrate wagons and a brake van totalling 1,036 tonnes, (1,020 tons) with a typical departure from Broken Hill at 11.30 for arrival at Parkes 03.24 the next

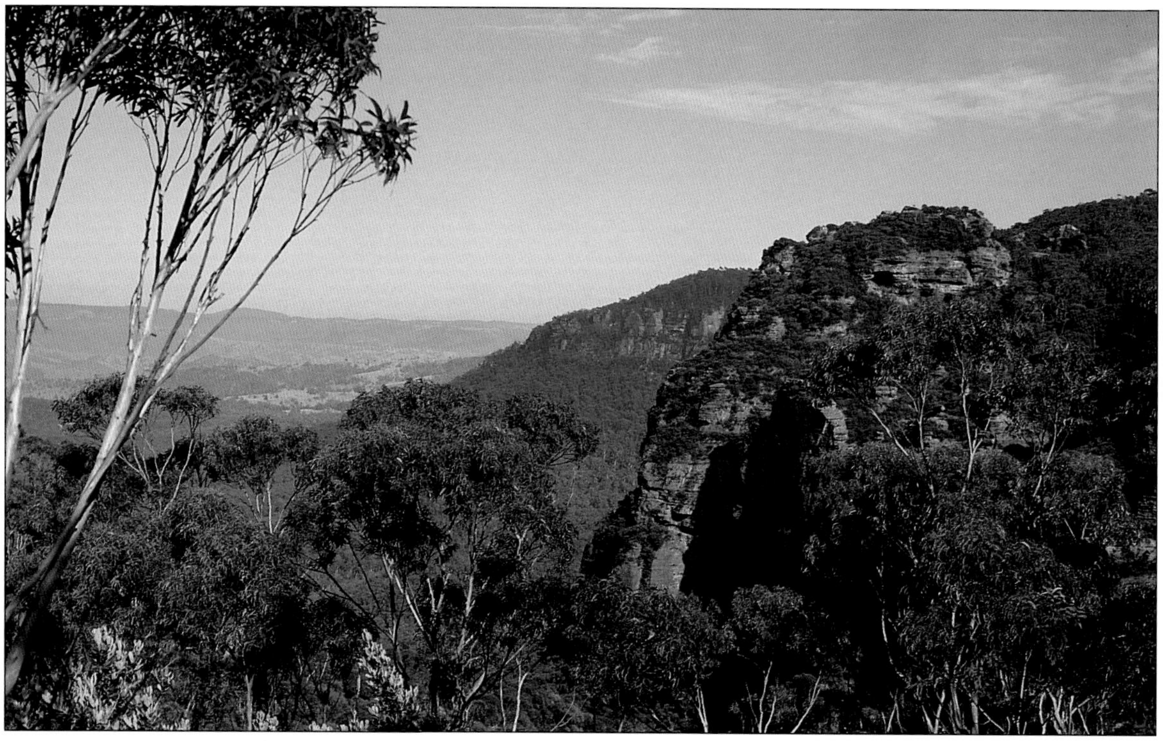

ABOVE
A New South Wales 3644 assists Garratt 6014 with a heavy Western goods at Borenore in 1966. Seventy-five of the 4-6-0 (C)36 Class, known affectionately as "Pigs", were built for express passenger-traffic from 1925 but ended their days on express goods. The 42 (AD)60 Class Garratts were the main goods power at the end of steam.

LEFT
The journey takes the traveller through the Blue Mountains National Park.

INFORMATION BOX

Termini	Broken Hill and Sulphide Junction
Country	Australia
Distance	1,252 km (778 miles)
Date of opening	1927

morning. Here the story changes as the diesel was replaced by a Garratt steam locomotive assisted by a "Standard Goods" Consolidation or a 36 Class 4-6-0 express locomotive relegated from passenger services. The train now faced a ruling grade of 1:60 to travel the 86 km (53 miles) to Molong in 3 hours and 20 minutes, arriving at 10.00. Here there was another change, as the assistant engine came off and was replaced by a modified Garratt. These modified units had enlarged cylinders, while the addition of duplicate controls allowed the crew to face the direction of running when working in reverse.

This new Garratt was attached with the bunker leading to remove the smoke nuisance later in the journey when working hard through the Marangaroo tunnel. At 10.35 the two monsters thundered through clouds of automotive dust towards the 1:40 grades *en route* to Orange East Folk. The modified Garratt then continued unaided to Bathers, received assistance up the Raglan Bank, and then went on alone again to Lithgow.

Lithgow is the beginning of the crossing of the Blue Mountains, and in earlier days the climb was started with a zigzag. This was replaced in 1911 by a double track through ten tunnels. Nevertheless, the start of the climb was 1:42 around an 8-chain (20 m/66 ft) curve, and prior to electrification heavy goods trains had two Standard Goods and NSW's most powerful non-articulated locomotive, the 57 Class Mountain, leading, with a further Standard Goods pushing from the rear – a sight and sound never to be surpassed.

W-44 had two 49 Class electric locomotives over this stretch, with one coming off at Newnes Junction and the remaining unit continuing onwards. At Katoomba, at the top of the 1:33 descending grade, the train was stopped and grade-control valves set before a safe journey down the mountains could be started. These grade-control valves permitted only a very slow release of the Westinghouse Brakes, giving the locomotive time to recharge the air reservoirs between brake applications on the long descent. On joining the Main Northern Line, an additional 46 Class assisted to the then end of electrification at Gosford. At 01.24 a modified Garratt with Standard Goods assistance departed on the final leg of the journey, arriving at Sulphide Junction at 03.28.

● **ABOVE**
One of the many fine views of the Blue Mountains to be experienced on the journey to Sulphide Junction.

● **RIGHT**
The final leg of the journey for the block train was on the Main Northern Line, but this section was run in darkness. Here another goods service on the same route sees a 60 Class Garratt taking over from a 46 Class electric locomotive just north of Gosford yard.

Ferntree Gully to Gembrook
Puffing Billy

The main routes radiating from the Victorian capital, Melbourne, were broad gauge. With the great depression of the 1890s, the Victorian government sought cheaper ways of handling the traffic in remoter parts of the State, with the result that four branch lines were built to 760 mm gauge for these areas. However, with the double handling of all freight and the coming of motor road vehicles, these lines soon became liabilities. Cutbacks and closures commenced in 1944, with services no longer running to Walhalla, and the final closure was that of the Beech Forest line in 1962.

The line from Upper Ferntree Gully to Gembrook was closest to Melbourne and became a popular tourist entry to the Dandenong Ranges. However, following several landslides about 10 km (6 miles) from Upper Ferntree Gully, railway services were abandoned from August 1953. The 29 km (18 mile) line had first been opened in December

INFORMATION BOX

PUFFING BILLY	
Termini	Ferntree Gully and Gembrook
Country	Australia
Distance	29 km (18 miles)
Date of opening	1900

● RIGHT
The Puffing Billy Preservation Society's 2-6-2T locomotive No. 7A crossing a curved wooden viaduct shortly after leaving Belgrave in Victoria, while hauling one of its regular tourist services into the Dandenong Ranges.

● OPPOSITE BELOW
There are many types of plants and flowers which can be seen from the train. One of these is the Olinda Rhodendron.

● OPPOSITE AND BELOW
Animals can also be seen such as the koala and the kangaroo.

1900, and with a speed limit of 24 kph (15 mph) the journey took two-and-a-quarter hours.

However, in December 1954, a Melbourne newspaper sponsored trips between Upper Ferntree Gully and Belgrave, about 5 km (3 miles) away, and following public demand further trips were run. In Easter of the following year, the Puffing Billy Preservation Society was formed with the aim of ensuring the retention of the fan trips. These lasted until February 1958 when, with the expansion of the Melbourne Metropolitan area, the Government decided to widen the gauge to Belgare and electrify the line.

The volunteers of the PBPS again went into battle to attempt to restore and re-open the balance of the abandoned line. Through the work of the volunteers, aided by the 3rd Field Engineer Regiment of the Citizen Military Forces, scouts etc., a new station and locomotive depot was built at Belgrave and the line restored to Menzies Creek, about 5 km (3 miles) away. This included a 2-chain (20 m/66 ft) radius deviation around the landslide, which had caused the closure of the line. Services recommenced in July 1962, and the society also established a museum at Menzies Creek.

Since then the society has grown in leaps and bounds, and work is in progress from both ends to complete the line once again to Gembrook. Passenger-traffic is heavy and growing, with most of it being handled by NA Class 2-6-2T locomotives, an 1898 American Baldwin design, although later engines of the same design were built locally. Also serviceable is a former timber line Climax, but this is too slow for regular traffic. The society owns a Victorian Railways narrow-gauge Garratt, and a South African Garratt has recently been acquired for conversion to 760 mm gauge to handle the growing traffic. New carriages are currently being built, so there is certainly confidence in the future. A Taiwanese Shay has been acquired for the museum, as well as a large variety of narrow-gauge locomotives from over Australia, which makes a visit well worth while.

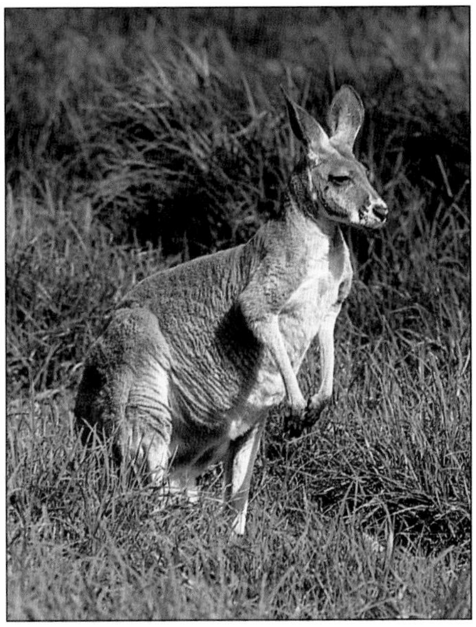

The route has a ruling grade of 1:30, limiting the load of the NA Class locomotives to 90 tonnes. Tight curves abound, and much of the country is heavily timbered. In places the suburban sprawl can be seen, and later a few farms. From Menzies Creek, the line descends to Clematis, once known as Paradise Valley, an area of rolling fields and stately homes, before the downhill run takes it to the banks of Emerald Lake and Lakeside, the current terminus for the tourist services. Unfortunately this part of Victoria has been subject to some disastrous bush fires, but the railway has survived and continues to progress.

Zeehan to Strahan
A West Coast Safari

Though the smallest state of Australia, Tasmania probably has the greatest variety of scenery, and any traveller thinking of assessing the State in a few days has much to learn. The north-west coast has a very English atmosphere about it, but heading southwards along the west coast we find rain forest in rugged mountainous country cut by deep ravines. This wild country, however, has meant more to Tasmania's economy than the rest of the State, for the area is rich in minerals, possessing huge deposits of tin, lead, silver, gold, copper and iron ores. As it is difficult country for road construction, access to the deposits was generally achieved by tramways or railways.

In its day Mount Bischoff was the largest tin mine in the world, and the Van Diemens Land Company connected the area to Burnie with a horse tramway in 1878. This was soon converted to a 1,067 mm gauge railway, the first 59 km (37 miles) now being the northern end of the private Emu Bay Railway.

Galena (lead sulphide) deposits were found at Zeehan, and transport for the silver was also needed. The Government was finally persuaded to construct a line to the coastal port of Strahan, and in 1892 this 46 km (28 mile) line with a ruling gauge of 1:40 was opened.

Meanwhile, huge copper ore deposits had been found at Mount Lyell, and by

INFORMATION BOX

Termini	Zeehan and Strahan
Country	Australia
Distance	46 km (28 miles)
Date of opening	1892

● **ABOVE**
The Mt Lyell Mining & Railway Company's line connecting their copper mine in Tasmania with the coast was through lush rain forest. This is a passenger's view ahead shortly before the line closed in 1963.

● **BELOW LEFT**
Tourists inspect the push-up engine, while the lead engine fills its tanks at the summit at Rinadeena.

● **BELOW RIGHT**
From the left, a tourist bus waits on a flat wagon to be shunted on to the train; a hired Tasmanian Railways diesel–mechanical locomotive waits with a goods-train bound for Zeehan; No. 6, an immaculate Dübs 4-8-0, and an Australian Standard Garratt waits with a goods-train that will follow behind.

● RIGHT
One of the problems leading to the closure of the Mt Lyell railway in Tasmania was the cost of maintenance on the "quarter mile bridge" over the King River, seen here being crossed by a Drewry diesel locomotive.

1899 the Mt Lyell Mining and Railway Company had constructed a tortuous but very scenic 34 km (21 mile) line of which 7 km (4½ miles) was operated on 1:16 and 1:20 grades on the Abt rack principle to Regatta Point near Strahan, a journey of two hours' duration. The Emu Bay Railway, seeing business potential in this area, pushed their line southwards through dense forests and over various streams to reach Zeehan, 142 km (88 miles) from Burnie, in 1901.

As the Government had connected Strahan to Regatta Point in 1900, it was then possible to travel all the way from Burnie on the north-west coast to Mount Lyell, using three different carriers. Owing to the light track, speeds were seldom in excess of 16 kph (10 mph), but in 1912 when a fire, caused by arsonists, occurred in the Mount Lyell mine with 170 men underground, the train racing breathing apparatus, rescue equipment and personnel to the mine cut five hours off the journey, resulting in the saving of many lives.

The copper and barytes from Mount Lyell was loaded on to shipping at Regatta Point, and the silver from Zeehan went on the Emu Bay railway, leaving the government line to decline rapidly, operated by one locomotive and a railcar. The line closed in 1960.

Tourism was growing on the west coast and the Mount Lyell Railway, probably the most scenic in Australia with its rack line over mountainous rain forest country and the King River gorge alongside, soon attracted its share. Unfortunately the owners and the Government still decided to close the line in 1963. Today, eight diesel-hydraulic locomotives coupled together bring in Mount Lyell ore between Zeehan and Roseberry. Tour trains periodically travel the line, and a Dübs locomotive is currently under restoration with a view to recreating the "West Coaster" express.

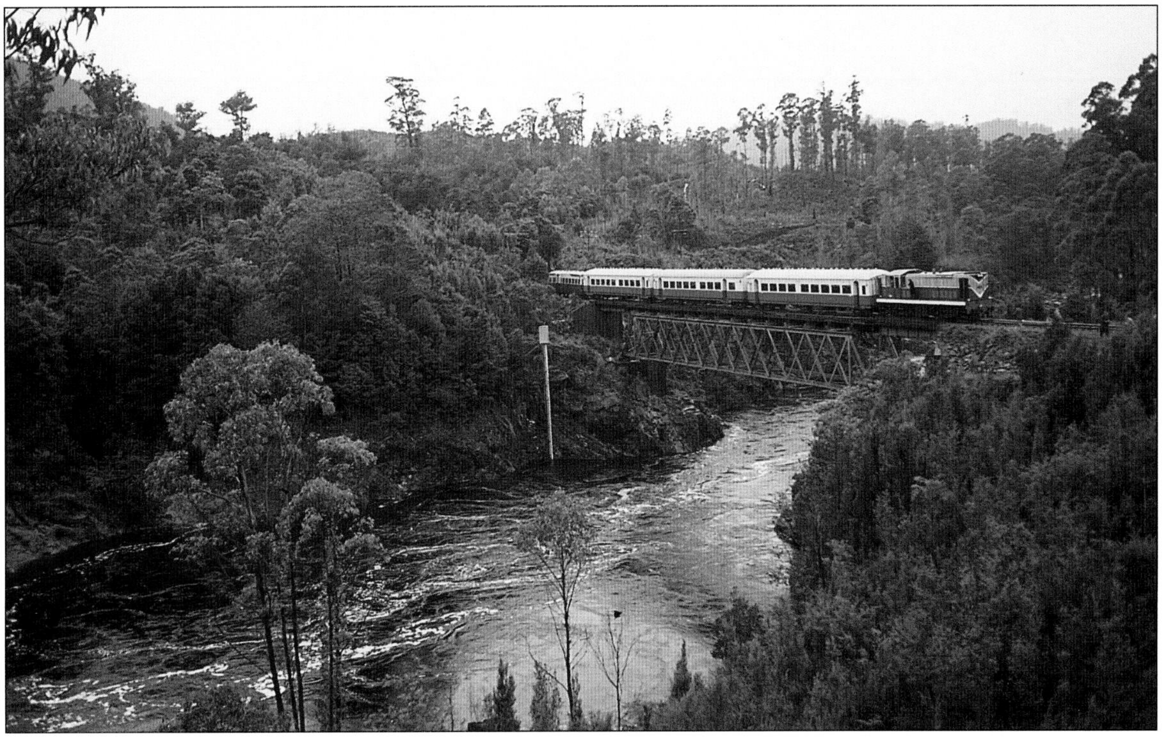

● RIGHT
Just north of Rosebery on the Emu Bay Railway in Tasmania was the Pieman River bridge, here being crossed by a tourist special of Tasmanian Railway's coaches in their "blood and custard" colours being hauled by a 10 Class BBR diesel-hydraulic loco-motive during Easter 1965. With the damming of the river for hydro-electric purposes, the line has since been deviated to higher ground and a new bridge built.

Pacific Coast Motorail

Since surfing became fashionable, a section of over 30 km (19 miles) of the Australian coastline just north of the New South Wales border from Coolangatta to Southport has been developed into the major holiday destination in Australia. Known as the Gold Coast, it caters for almost all levels of society, the temperate climate allowing it to be a resort all the year round.

Queenslanders had had access by a narrow-gauge train for many years, but, owing to the slow service, buses soon won this traffic and the line closed. However, with the Brisbane suburban electrification, a new line is being opened along part of the length of the coast.

The big influx of tourists come from the south – New South Wales and Victoria – though direct transport has been slow in coming to feed this area. Prior to the mid-1920s, Sydneysiders had to travel north to Brisbane by the main northern line, which crossed to the west of the Great Dividing Range. Then they continued to the Queensland border, well inland from the coast, where a change was made to the narrow gauge to cross the Great Divide again and descend to Brisbane, where another train was caught to the Gold Coast.

The Clarence River was the main obstacle to a coastal journey. An isolated section of railway had been built from Lismore via Byron Bay to Murwillumbah, about 32 km (20 miles) south of the border on the coast, prior to the turn of the century, but it was not until 1924 that the two sections of coastal line faced each other across the Clarence River at Grafton and a train ferry service was introduced. Although the standard-gauge track reached Brisbane in September 1930, the ferry continued until May 1932, when a double-deck road-rail bridge was built over the river.

The Department of Railways, however, did not see an early need for

ABOVE
Hauled by two 442 Class locomotives, the Pacific Coast Motorail heads north from Lismore. The locomotives and the sitting cars at the end of the train are in a short-lived "candy" colour scheme, while the power car and sleeping cars are of stainless steel.

LEFT
With the elimination of almost all locomotive hauled passenger-trains in NSW, the Pacific Coast Motorail was superseded by the XPTs. Here an XPT charges through regrowth timber country near Bonville in northern New South Wales.

● **RIGHT**
The 1990s saw the introduction of XPT inter-city services, speeding up the timetable considerably. Not only was the speed limit raised to 160 kph (100 mph) but also many of the smaller stopping-places were closed. Here we see a southbound XPT crossing Boambee Creek between the coastal resorts of Coffs Harbour and Sawtell.

● **BELOW**
The southbound Pacific Coast Motorail approaching Lismore.

more direct traffic to the Gold Coast, and intending travellers had to catch the Brisbane Express and change trains at the crack of dawn for a branch-line service to Murwillumbah, where a bus would complete the journey. Eventually the traffic potential of the holiday seekers was realized, and in the early 1970s a through service to Murwillumbah was introduced, which included car carriers for those wishing to travel around the extensive holiday area. This was known as the Gold Coast Motorail.

Whether owing to interstate jealousies or a desire to promote the northern coast of New South Wales, in the 1980s the train also unloaded cars *en route* at Casino and was renamed the Pacific Coast Motorail. Today, with the almost complete elimination of locomotive-hauled passenger-trains, this service has gone. Now an XPT service runs the route, with a bus connection at Murwillumbah.

The Motorail service, with sleeping cars, departed Sydney at 06.25 with the first light of dawn creeping over at somewhere near Coffs Harbour. Here the mountains come almost to the coast, and the huge banana plantations, which cover the hillsides, could be seen from the train between the various tunnels.

The train turned inland and ran through hilly and well-timbered country northwards to reach South Grafton, a former meal-stop, where it crossed the river and continued north through undulating timber country to the town of Casino. Then came Byron Bay, the easternmost point of Australia. Further north, sugar cane country was entered, before the train finally descended to the Tweed River at Murwillumbah, where it arrived at 13.05.

INFORMATION BOX

Termini	Sydney and Murwillumbah
Country	Australia
Length	935 km (581 miles)
Date of opening	1932

Christchurch to Greymouth
The Transalpine Route

New Zealand is not well known for its railways. This is a shame, as some of the scenery traversed is the equal of anywhere else. The 233 km (145 mile) long Midland line is probably the most scenic route in New Zealand. Construction, by the English-financed New Zealand Midland Railway Company, commenced in 1885.

Unfortunately progress was slow and after ten years, with only about 60 km (37 miles) in service, the Government took possession of the line and continued its construction. In those days, with limited engineering equipment available, the most difficult task was the boring of the tunnel section from Arthur's Pass to Otira. After much consideration of alternative ways of crossing the mountain range this 8.6 km ($5^1/2$ mile) long tunnel, with a descent at 1:33 from Arthur's Pass to Otira, was started in August 1908, but was only opened almost 15 years to the day later on 4 August 1923.

It had been a very difficult bore, with World War I adding to the problems that nature imposed. At the time of its opening, this tunnel was claimed to be the seventh longest in the world. With such a steep grade in such a long tunnel, working heavy trains through by steam was most uncomfortable, not to say dangerous, and so the tunnel was electrified at 1,500 volts d.c., and five Bo-Bo locomotives were imported from the English Electric Company.

This tunnel, however, was not the only one along the route. Another 16 tunnels occur in a very short section near Staircase along the scenic gorge of the Waimakiri River, as do many spectacular viaducts and bridges, and a further two tunnels at the western end of the line.

Commencing a journey from Christchurch, a little over the first hour of the trip is spent travelling over the Canterbury Plains *en route* to Springfield, 71 km (44 miles) away. From here the Alps come into view and the line follows the Waimakariri River in its spectacular gorge. Four large viaducts and 16 tunnels are features of the next section to Avoca, 97 km (60 miles) from Christchurch. Soon mountain ranges become visible, and the line parts company with the Waimakariri River a little before Cora Lynn, 125 km (78 miles) from the start of the journey.

From here the train enters Arthur's Pass National Park, a popular tourist destination throughout the year. Arthur's

● LEFT
Between Otira and Arthur's Pass on the Transalpine route is an 8.6 km ($5^1/2$ mile) long tunnel on a 1:33 grade. To assist trains through the tunnel, three Toshiba Bo-Bo electric locomotives working in multiple are used through the tunnel. At Arthur's Pass the threesome prepare for the next journey.

● LEFT
In 1923, to make more bearable the passage through the 8.6 km ($5^1/2$ mile) long Otira tunnel, with its 1:33 grade, New Zealand Railways electrified the tunnel. With the original electric locomotives worn out, five replacement Bo-Bo units of 1286 hp were obtained from Toshiba in Japan. Normally these locomotives worked in threes, one being spare and one in the workshops for servicing. Here they are seen at the Arthur's Pass end of the tunnel.

● **LEFT**
The Transalpine route across the South Island follows the Waimakariri River for a considerable portion of the journey. This view is taken from the train.

INFORMATION BOX	
Termini	Christchurch and Greymouth
Country	New Zealand
Distance	233 km (145 miles)
Date of opening	1923

Pass station, at an elevation of 737 m (2,418 ft), is the highest station in the South Island of New Zealand. Once through the Otira tunnel, rivers and lakes are a feature of the continuing scenery. Coral mining activity is evident near the west coast, as the gold rush that sparked interest in the west coast never really happened. At Greymouth, on the west coast, the present-day journey ends some 4 hours and 25 minutes after leaving Christchurch.

From 1939, in steam days, much of the traffic was handled by New Zealand's most powerful non-articulated locomotives, the Kb Class. Through the Otira tunnel the trains were hauled, generally triple-headed, by electric Eo Class locomotives. These old electrics were replaced in 1968 by five new Toshiba units, which are also worked with three coupled together. Steam had now been replaced by Mitsubishi diesel-electrics with a Bo-Bo-Bo wheel arrangement. These units are powered by Caterpillar diesels and are rated at 670kV.

● **ABOVE RIGHT**
Diesel electric locomotive Dj-1218 crossing the Kowai viaduct. This is the first viaduct on the Transalpine route, just before the railway enters the Waimakariri gorge.

● **RIGHT**
Dj 1218 hauls a tourist train across the Broken River viaduct on the Transalpine route. The view on one side of the train is unfortunately blocked out by the windshield needed to prevent trains being blown off the bridge in bad weather.

CHRISTCHURCH TO WELLINGTON – *THE COASTAL PACIFIC EXPRESS*

● ABOVE
The old "colonial" style is nicely represented in this street in Christchurch.

● BELOW
The sea reflects the blue of the sky in this placid scene near Christchurch.

The route from Christchurch to Wellington travels through spectacular scenery which is the equal of anywhere else in the world. In 1991, there were only long-distance passenger services operating over five routes, and only one of these, Wellington to Auckland, had more than one train each way per day. In addition, Auckland and Wellington have commuter railways, the latter electrified. Subsequently, New Zealand Railways (NZR) has been taken over by Wisconsin Rail of the USA (who have also taken over most of the UK freight operation under the name English, Welsh & Scottish Railways).

This train journey is from Christchurch to Wellington by the Coastal Pacific Express. More accurately, it goes to Picton, from where the railway-owned inter-island ferry must be taken to reach Wellington. This journey exemplifies the problem facing long-haul services in New Zealand, for it takes nine-and-a-half hours by rail and boat, but only one hour by air. There is only limited consolation in the fact that the roads are not much quicker.

The journey starts from Christchurch station, a big 1960s building on a large site, both echoing the past rather than the drastically reduced present. Two of NZR's other passenger services also start from here, the Trans-Alpine Express going over Arthur's Pass in the New Zealand Alps to Greymouth and the Southerner Express to Dunedin and Invercargill.

Christchurch was home to one of the four areas of electrified railways in New Zealand, the short and now dieselized route through the tunnel to the nearest port at Lyttelton. The other electrified sections, all remaining, are the summit tunnel at Arthur's Pass, the central section of the Wellington to Auckland main line (the North Island Trunk) and the Wellington suburban network.

The Coastal Pacific follows the South Island Trunk, as it hugs the eastern side of the South Island. This line took a long time to build, as it was affected not only by the difficult terrain to be crossed, but

RIGHT
Diesel locomotive DF 6162 at the head of the Coastal Pacific Express at Kaikoura. Thirty 1,230 kW locomotives was delivered by General Motors Canada in 1979–80.

also by various communities each preferring different routes. The current general route was decided upon in 1883, although the first section along this route had been opened in 1872. The final detail of the route was revised several times until the late 1930s. The through route was only completed in December 1945, when the section between Parnassus and Wharanui was opened. The further delays had been brought about by two world wars and economic depressions, both local and global. The track is laid to 3 ft 6 in Cape Gauge, although some early sections had been laid initially with a gauge of 5 ft 3 in. Although only around 100 km (60 miles) of the 348 km (216 miles) is by the sea, it is visions of the rugged scenery on this section that remain in the mind of the rail traveller.

The railborne part of the journey takes 5 hours and 20 minutes to reach Picton, where there is a 50-minute connection into the "Interislander" ferry.

ABOVE
South-east of Blenheim there are views from the train of Cook Strait, with the North Island visible in the distance. The railway curves around to pass through the cutting in the centre of the picture.

LEFT
A view of coastline from the train south of Kaikoura. The route of the railway and coastal road can be seen hugging the coastline around the promontory.

INFORMATION BOX

Termini	Christchurch and Wellington
Country	New Zealand
Distance	348 km (216 miles)
Date of opening	1945

● LEFT
Diesel shunting locomotive DSJ 4032 at Picton. This class of five locomotives was designed by Toshiba in Japan, where the first one was built. The other four were erected from imported parts in NZR's Addington workshops in 1984.

The train consists of three coaches and a baggage van hauled by a DF Class diesel locomotive. The coaches are a batch of vehicles modernized for what amount to tourist services introduced in September 1988 by enlarging the windows, covering the seats with lambswool, installing a public address system etc. They were painted in the long-distance passenger-coach livery of blue with red-and-white stripes. There is a hostess aboard the train, giving a commentary on the history of the line and various sites to be seen from the train. Cream teas are available as part of the food service, along with cold snacks and a bar service. This innovation obviated the need for the trains to make long stops at certain stations to allow passengers to visit the refreshment rooms, a practice that had continued right up until introduction of the Coastal Pacific.

Leaving Christchurch, the route crosses flat farmland before entering the rolling hill country of North Canterbury. The foothills of the central mountain range are visible almost immediately. Soon the traveller becomes aware of a recurring feature of the journey, the crossing of the estuaries of rivers flowing down from the Southern Alps into the Pacific Ocean. Some of these estuaries are very wide and require long viaducts to take the railway across. The Ashley River, 35 km (22 miles) from Christchurch and the second river crossing, is one of the longest at 549 m (1,801 ft). After around 80 km (50 miles), the train reaches the highest point on the line, 135 m (443 ft) above sea level, at Spye. Just before Parnassus, the 706 m (2,316 ft) bridge crossing the Waiau River is the longest on this route.

● RIGHT
Gorse frequently provides a startling splash of colour on the journey to Christchurch.

● BELOW
The Cook Strait lives up to its reputation for rough seas.

● RIGHT
Picton station building. Note the old railway vans being given a new lease of life off the track.

The Pacific coastal section, between Claverley and Wharanui is very attractive, hugging the rocky shore and including 20 tunnels in its 100 km (60 miles). The statistics for this stretch of line (plus the stretch to Parnassus) give some idea of the work involved – there are 43 bridges totalling 3.2 km (2 miles) in length; 2.9 million cubic metres (102 million cubic feet) of rock and spoil had to be excavated; and between Goose Bay and Kowhai the road had to be extended over the beach to make way for the railway. Hawkeswood cutting, just north of Parnassus is, at over one kilometre (⅔ mile) long and up to 19 m (62 ft) deep, the largest in New Zealand. It is near here that the train passes from Canterbury into Marlborough on crossing the Conway River.

After leaving the coast, the railway crosses the salt lakes of Lake Grasmere on a causeway. The section on to Blenheim includes a double-deck viaduct

● LEFT
DX 5500 stands at the head of a short main-line train with coaches in an attractive blue livery. Behind it, in this scene at Wellington, is the "Silver Fern" express railcar.

● LEFT
A local train formed of a two-car EMU waits for passengers at Wellington.

● BELOW
New livery on an electric multiple unit at Wellington.

near Seddon to cross the Awatere River, where the railway track takes the top deck, and the road takes the lower.

After Blenheim the line passes into one of New Zealand's major wine-producing areas. A little way north of Blenheim is the 293 m (961 ft) bridge across the Wairau River. The stretch through hills to Picton crosses the 129 m (423 ft) Waitohi viaduct, once the largest timber trestle bridge in the country, but now a concrete bridge. Picton, a small town that has flourished as a result of being the port for the inter-island ferry, is approached on a 1:37 gradient, the steepest on the route. This gradient is a result of the town's picturesque setting, surrounded by large hills, which form a major barrier for the railway.

Most stations no longer have freight facilities as a result of transport deregulation in the 1980s, and rail business is now dominated by container traffic. The increasing power available from newer locomotives is allowing an increase in train weights and a reduction in the number of services.

The inter-island roll-on, roll-off ferries were introduced in 1962, with management passing to NZR in 1971. This service is marketed as the "Interislander". The four crossings each way per day carry road and rail vehicles and form an integral part of the New Zealand railways freight network.

The port of Picton is a fair way from the open sea, on a side fjord off the Queen Charlotte Sound. While this does not have the towering mountainsides that the name suggests – for that one should visit Milford Sound on the south-west corner of the South Island – the hilly

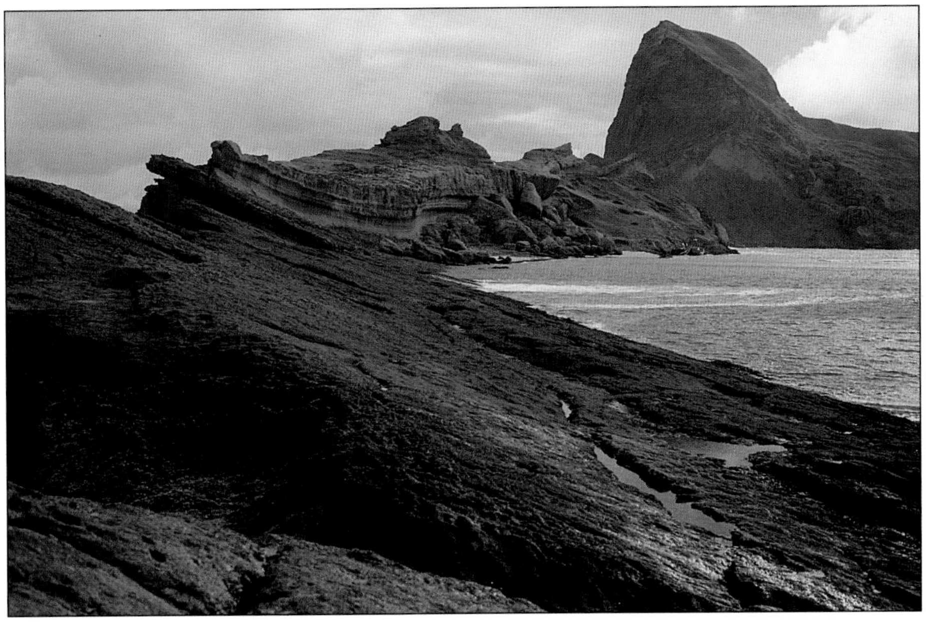

country around the watercourse is attractive. Nearer the sea, seals can often be seen sunning themselves on the rocks.

The boat journey across the Cook Strait takes 3 hours and 20 minutes for the 52 nautical miles (96 km). One of the ferries used is the *Aratika*, originally built in France in 1974 as a train ferry but converted in 1976 to carry cars and passengers along with rail wagons.

While the approach to Wellington is by no means as scenic as the departure from Picton, it gives a different view of the city, the central area of which is steep enough to warrant a (Swiss-built) funicular. Foot passengers are met on the quay at Wellington by the "Interislander" shuttle bus and taken to the bus station outside Wellington railway station.

Anyone visiting New Zealand should try to make time to travel the Coastal Pacific Express. The scenery alone is worth the time; the glimpses of the "real" New Zealand, away from the tourist areas, are a bonus.

● **ABOVE**
The impressive rocky coastline at Castle Point near Wellington is a popular spot for visitors.

● **BELOW**
The attractive coastline near Wellington is further embellished by a geyser.

PICTON TO CHRISTCHURCH
THE COASTAL PACIFIC EXPRESS

Historically, the important commercial centre of Wellington, on New Zealand's North Island, has been linked to the city of Christchurch – seat of provincial government and gateway to the vast agricultural hinterland of Canterbury – on the South Island, by a network of coastal steamers.

The first proposal for a rail line to join the two was mooted in 1861. A broad-gauge line was commenced northwards under the auspices of the Provincial Government in 1872. It was later converted to 3 ft 6 in gauge in 1877. A line southwards from Picton was opened in 1875. Further construction followed as resources and political decisiveness permitted, but, even by 1916, the northern line had reached only so far as Wharanui, 90 km (56 miles) from Picton, while the southern section penetrated as far as Parnassus, 133 km (83 miles) from Christchurch. It was to be another 20 years before meaningful progress was made in closing the gap, through the fearsome mountainous terrain around Kaikoura. The line opened throughout officially on 15 December 1945.

In 1954, a rail roll-on, roll-off ferry altered the connecting sea crossing and, in 1988, the service was transformed by the introduction of rebuilt rolling stock. The trip provides four main features of

● **BELOW LEFT**
Centre cab shunters exchange wagons between ship and shore.

INFORMATION BOX

THE COASTAL PACIFIC EXPRESS

Termini	Picton and Christchurch
Country	New Zealand
Distance	rail 348 km (216 miles); sea crossing 80 km (50 miles)
Date of opening	1945

● **LEFT**
No. 6110 at the head of the southbound Coastal Pacific Express at Picton. The locomotive is a DF Class Co-Co built by General Motors, Canada, in 1979 and is rated at 1250 kW.

● RIGHT
Atanaga, an "Interislander" ferry, makes an impressive sight as she proceeds up the now sheltered waters toward Picton, South Island.

interest. After the sea crossing, memorable in itself, comes the ride through the hills of Marlborough, followed by the exhilarating passage through the harsher mountains around Kaikoura with the Pacific Ocean as an intimate companion, and finally the gentler landscape leading towards Canterbury Plain.

After the passage across the exposed waters of the Cook Strait, one enters the comparatively sheltered area of the Marlborough Sound. Here there is a multitude of islands and islets, some little more than wave-washed rocks, others massive crags or verdant mounds. Wildlife is abundant.

The final passage to the port in its sheltered setting is almost serene after the earlier bluster. The community of Picton, with its jetty, rail and freight yards and low-rise housing, is dominated by the surrounding ridges and peaks, not unlike a port serving the Western Isles of Scotland.

One can watch the unloading and loading of railway traffic from the ferry if one wishes or, perhaps more prudently, retrieve one's baggage from the somewhat unsupervised free-for-all below. Once rightful ownership is secured, there is time to survey the train that will provide the rest of the journey.

● LEFT
Even in the partial shelter of Marlborough Sound, islets and cliffs are assaulted by wave and wind.

● BELOW LEFT
The deep cutting in Dashwood Pass is seen from further up the line. It forms part of an 8 km (5 mile), 1:53 climb.

The concept of a "luxury" service on the route had followed the successful introduction of a similar service between Christchurch and Greymouth through the alpine scenery of South Island. Several existing coaches were converted, receiving large (2 m x 1 m; 6 ft 6 in x 1 ft 4 in) panoramic windows, separated by narrow pillars, that provide excellent visibility. The seats, which face each other in pairs across a large snack table either side of the central aisle, have high backs and are sumptuously furnished in sheepskin. Wall to wall carpeting, large ventilators, curtains and an effective public address system furnish an attractive environment. Internal colours are pink and grey, while the external livery is mid-blue relieved by white-and-red bands. A buffet car provides both snacks and a full bar service. Uniformed attendants and a well-informed

● LEFT
Road and rail share the narrow coastal strip between Pacific breakers and mountains, which proved such an obstacle to the construction of the line.

conductor making sensible use of the PA all add to the ambience of the journey.

Once everyone is aboard, the train winds out of Picton and commences a steep 1:37 climb, and rumbles across the sweeping 129 m (423 ft) Waitohi viaduct. The town, itself originally known as Waitohi, is overshadowed by tumbling tree-clad foothills, jumbled peaks and the waters of the sound. By Elevation, 4 km ($2^1/_2$ miles) from Picton, the mountains take on an Italianate or Austrian alpine air, with strands of conifer and dusty logging tracks, but the pastures below with their scattered specimen trees owe more to English parkland, albeit with trees unfamiliar to visitors.

Before Blenheim, the train passes the blue waters and gravel banks of the Wairau on a long low bridge. Blenheim itself serves as the gateway to the increasingly well-known wine growing regions of Marlborough. Beyond Blenheim, the train commences yet another long ascent, this time towards the bleaker regions of Dashwood Pass, the 8 km (5 mile) 1:53 climb being presaged by a sweeping horseshoe curve. The mountains here are softened by the effects of the elements into smooth folds rather than pronounced peaks, the more sheltered pockets offering a refuge for isolated clumps of low trees.

Another grade takes the train to the unusual bridge over the Awatere River. This is a combination bridge with the railway carried on an upper deck and the road below. The next point of note on the trip is Blind River, the site of the worst crash on the line in 1948 when six people were killed. The train then crosses over a long causeway, the vast salt lakes on the approach to Lake Grasmere.

Near Wharanui, the long stretch of coastal running begins. From here the traveller can enjoy some one-and-a-half hours of superb scenery before the stop at Kaikoura. For much of the way, railway and road are squeezed into a narrow strip between beach and mountain. In the approximately 100 km (62 miles) of line to Oaro there are 20 tunnels, numerous embankments and steep cuttings, sharp curves and lonely bridges, of which there are more than 40 along the central section of line. One stretch of track, known as the "Blue Slip", is notorious for the highly unstable nature of the ground through which it passes in cutting: the local rock of blue pug absorbs water easily, and the whole hillside is heading slowly for the sea.

As gullies come down to the sea and the train speeds on, there are glimpses of remote valleys, sheltering between flowing hills and rising gently to more majestic and mysterious mountains. The sinuous course of the line, which follows the indentations of the sea, is interrupted

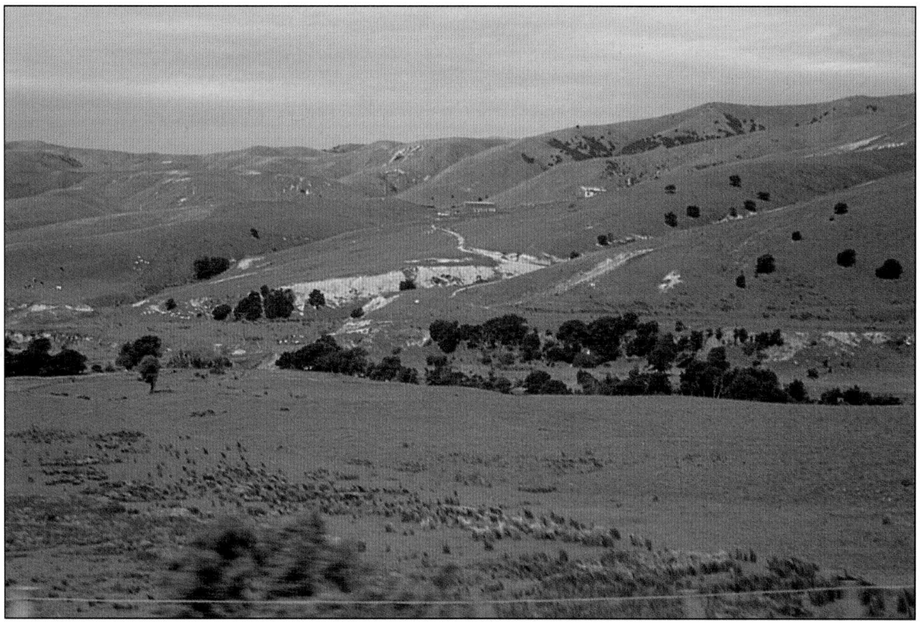

● **RIGHT**
Passengers take the opportunity to stretch their legs during the stop at the attractive intermediate station of Kaikoura.

as Kaikoura – its name is said to be from the Maori *kai* (food) and *koura* (crayfish) – is approached. This fishing centre and former whaling community lies on a peninsula about half-way between Picton and Christchurch.

Here the train pauses long enough for passengers to alight from the train and stretch their legs, a reminder of when it needed to stop for refreshments. Onboard buffet facilities now make such an extended halt redundant, but the old building is still there and retains much of its former charm.

Leaving the town on another curving viaduct, there is a further period of spectacular coastal running with a stretch of line with nine tunnels in as many kilometres. Beyond Oaro, at sea level again, the train climbs steeply and encounters the almost kilometre (2/3 mile) long tunnel at Amuri Bluff and the adjacent Okarahia viaduct. Soon the suburbs of Christchurch come into view and this spectacular journey is sadly over.

● **ABOVE RIGHT**
Canterbury has seen many architectural styles, and as yet traffic has not reached the urban levels found elsewhere.

● **OPPOSITE**
Clumps of low trees find sheltered pockets in the windswept hills beyond Blenheim.

● **RIGHT**
The ferry port of Picton on South Island nestles in the lee of mountains at the head of Marlborough Sound.

INDEX

● ABOVE
A Fujikawa express train at Shimobe. Shimobe -Onsen is a principal station and most trains, including the Fujikawa expresses, stop here.